MANIPURATED

*How Business Owners Can Fight Fraudulent
Online Ratings and Reviews*

by Daniel Lemin

Fresno, California

Manipurated
How Business Owners Can Fight Fraudulent
Online Ratings and Reviews

Copyright © 2015 by Daniel Lemin. All rights reserved.

Excerpt from Tripadvisor.com, © 2014, TripAdvisor, LLC.
All rights Reserved. Used with Permission.

Published by Quill Driver Books,
an imprint of Linden Publishing
2006 South Mary, Fresno, California 93721
559-233-6633 / 800-345-4447
QuillDriverBooks.com

Quill Driver Books and Colophon
are trademarks of Linden Publishing, Inc.

ISBN 978-1-61035-262-8

Printed in the United States
First Printing

Library of Congress Cataloging-in-Publication Data

Names: Lemin, Daniel, author.
Title: Manipurated : how business owners can fight fraudulent online
   ratings and reviews / by Daniel Lemin.
Description: Fresno, California : Quill Driver Books, [2015] |
Includes index.
Identifiers: LCCN 2015034210 | ISBN 9781610352628 (pbk. :
   alk. paper)
Subjects: LCSH: Internet in public relations. | Customer relations. |
   Public opinion. | Reputation. | Internet marketing. | Business
   enterprises--Ratings and rankings.
Classification: LCC HD59 .L46 2015 | DDC 659.2--dc23
LC record available at http://lccn.loc.gov/2015034210

Contents

Foreword

We believe each other.

Research from Nielsen shows that 91 percent of Americans trust recommendations from friends and family members.[1] That statistic is remarkable and makes me think, "Maybe other people have a more discerning group of friends and family members than I do."

But even more shocking is that 88 percent of consumers trust anonymous reviews as much as they trust personal recommendations.

Reviews.

Not from a friend, nor a family member, but from a stranger. Some guy who just happens to also like lattes and uses the same ratings website or mobile app that you do.

We believe him. We put our faith in his latte critiques. His rating —combined with our belief in it—has a material and measurable impact on the success or failure of the business that made that latte.

If it feels sometimes as though your business is a marionette being made to dance by customers holding all the strings with their ratings and reviews, you're right.

Public customer feedback is more important than ever, and there's a lot more of it as well. In the United Kingdom, complaints about businesses in social media nearly doubled between 2014 and 2015.[2]

It's hard to run a great business when you have to spend so much time monitoring and defending its reputation. You know that. I know that. And my friend and colleague Daniel Lemin, the author of this exceptional book, certainly knows that.

---

1 www.nielsen.com/us/en/insights/news/2009/global-advertising-consumers-trust-real-friends-and-virtual-strangers-the-most.html
2 www.telegraph.co.uk/news/shopping-and-consumer-news/11398974/British-shoppers-complain-more-than-ever.html

But the proliferation of ratings and reviews and their burgeoning ability to drive customers through your door—or away from it—are actually good news.

Most customers don't expect you, the business owner, to play this online game. They don't expect you to pay attention. They don't expect you to care about ratings and reviews—not really. In fact, research that I conducted for my book *Hug Your Haters* found that less than half of the consumers who complain on a reviews site expect a response. Less than half! With just a little bit of effort you can blow their minds and win their hearts.

There are smart businesspeople like you who understand how important consumer feedback can be. This book is for you. This book is for the people who want to master the nuances of the reviews landscape and use that understanding as a massive competitive differentiator.

But it isn't easy. The investigations and interviews Daniel Lemin conducted for this book opened my eyes, and they'll open yours, too. The rating-and-review ecosystem combines the best (and worst) of the Wild West, Las Vegas, and direct democracy, where every citizen has a voice.

Can you keep and create customers by getting more good reviews, and reducing bad ones? Absolutely. But to do so, you need to understand what's *really* going on with ratings and reviews. And as this book demonstrates, the inner workings are more complex, and at times nefarious, than we think.

What I love most about *Manipurated* is that even though it shines a bright spotlight on the tricky and troubling elements of ratings and reviews, it recognizes the inevitable importance of consumer feedback.

Daniel and I have worked together for many years. He is a straight shooter and a truth teller. In these pages, he shows you exactly how to succeed in this crazy, modern world where every customer has an opinion and the opportunity to share it in an instant. But he also shows you how to not get "manipurated," and that's advice and counsel needed by every business, everywhere.

—*Jay Baer*
Digital business expert, global keynote speaker, and author of Youtility

Introduction

• •

"I feel like they've stacked the cards against me," bemoaned Bobby Boas. Like you, Bobby is a business owner, and you will find his story (which is detailed in Chapter 1) hits close to home.

Bobby wasn't talking about negotiating his lease, drumming up financing, recruiting staff, or teaching himself business tax rules. He'd conquered all that. What exasperated him most about running his business was the ongoing uncertainty of his online ratings and reviews.

For business owners like Bobby, the online rating-and-review playing field feels like a pinball machine where you and your business are the pinball. Whether you wish to play or not, you're unwittingly thrust into a minefield designed with hidden traps and loops, your reputation batted around by random pushes of a button, and your emotions and business prospects erratically teetering in the wake.

Managing your business reputation didn't always feel so frenetic and out of your control. Before the rise of online ratings and reviews (ah, the good old days), customer feedback—good and bad—was a mostly one-on-one affair. Customers communicated complaints or praise to you directly, giving you the chance to respond appropriately.

With the rise of online ratings and reviews, businesses now confront websites that allow virtually anyone to say anything about your business to everyone on the Internet, regardless of truth or fairness. Though the discussion is about you, you're left feeling shut out of it.

And what if the comments are unfair, damaging, or even untrue? In cases where your business is threatened or harmed by such comments, there's little the rating-and-review industry will do to help you, even though it is making billions of dollars off the backs of businesses like yours.

You've picked up *Manipurated*, so I know you relate to what I'm talking about. You're probably facing your own crisis with the online rating-and-review industry—be it addressing bad reviews, figuring out how to manage your online rating-and-review profile\, or better yet, planning a strategy for turning the tables to make the platform work in *your* favor, not against you.

In this book, I'll show you how to achieve all of this. I have worked in the search and technology industry since 1999 and spent a considerable amount of time early in my career at Google. I've seen businesses like Bobby's and yours be continually challenged and threatened by the fast-evolving and mercurial rules of the technology industry. Those who figure out the rules and adapt early are apt to succeed; those who adapt slowly face tougher prospects.

In Part One of this book, I teach you the key players and rules of online ratings and reviews, how this platform developed, and the inner workings of this murky industry. This understanding helps you play the long game.

In Part Two, I outline an insider's toolkit packed with effective, practical, and actionable steps that you can implement *right now* to gain the upper hand.

Manipurated will show you how to transform the rating-and-review platform to your advantage by robustly inserting the needs of your business into the online conversation. No longer will you feel powerless!

Getting Back to Your Passion

As a small business owner like Bobby, you started your business to pursue a passion—whether it's cutting hair, feeding people, grooming pets, or providing a service for your community. The chances are that for most of you, that passion is probably not online rating-and-review marketing.

Helping you understand this industry is *my* passion. I have used the knowledge and techniques in this book to coach some of the world's largest brands. The investment you make now in learning how to skillfully navigate this industry will reward you and your business forever.

My goal is for you to experience successful results and peace of mind when dealing with online ratings and reviews. Ultimately, I hope this confidence will empower you to get back to your passion of building the business that inspires you.

Part One: Getting the Lay of the Land

How did the online rating-and-review industry gain so much influence over businesses? Part One of *Manipurated* answers this critical question. In the next few chapters, you are about to get deep under the hood of this industry and gain an insider's understanding of the nuts and bolts of what makes this powerful machine tick.

This part of the book is fast-paced and stuffed with case studies that will explain the frustration and fear you may be feeling, open your eyes to the real nature of the rating-and-review industry, and empower you with knowledge to effectively fight back.

If you have the time, I suggest you read through all of Part One to improve your background understanding. However, if you are pressed for time, I've provided some shortcuts below to help you get straight to the content that will set you down the right path.

Shortcuts

☞ Trying to understand why rating-and-review sites feel unfair and stacked against you? Then start with Chapter 1 (page 2).

☞ Where did the rating-and-review industry as we know it today come from? The answer might surprise you. Find out in Chapter 2 (page 11).

☞ Get a better understanding for how rating-and-review sites create a conflict of interest in Chapter 3 (page 24).

☞ Explore how the rating-and-review industry is failing businesses in Chapter 4 (page 32).

☞ See how focusing on rating-and-review sites, despite their many flaws, can boost your business in Chapter 5 (page 48).

1

Main Street Under Siege

In 2008, at the rock bottom of the Great Recession, Bobby Boas was at a crossroads in his career and decided to take an entrepreneurial leap.

A decade earlier, he had graduated from art school and embarked on an unexpectedly turbulent career in animation. His timing wasn't great— LA's animation job market was fiercely competitive and shrinking rapidly. Those years were stressful, unpredictable, and far less fulfilling than he had hoped. In that short period of time, and through no fault of his own, Bobby had been laid off (downsized, to use corporate speak) and left to settle for a string of part-time gigs.

In this chapter, you'll learn:

✔ Ways online rating-and-review sites harm businesses just like yours

✔ How being "manipurated" can sabotage all of your marketing efforts

✔ The top three complaints business owners have about rating-and-review sites

✔ Why apathy is not an option and how to begin developing your strategy

Meanwhile, Bobby had also been pursuing a budding passion on the side—hair. He discovered a zeal for styling hair and developed a true gift for the craft. He found himself wrapping up his animation day job and then working evenings cutting hair for friends and family. The positive feedback he consistently received and the pride he felt improving how people looked made Bobby realize he had found his vocational calling. Through word-of-mouth referrals, the self-taught stylist's client base grew quickly.

As his personal interest and prospects for full-time work in animation faded, Bobby followed his heart and decided to embark on a new career. He completed his beauty licensing, quit his animation job, and became a full-time hair stylist.

At first, Bobby worked for various well-regarded salons where he quickly learned the ropes of the business. Over time, however, he grew frustrated with how poorly managed, and at times even downright dysfunctional, the salons were. Bobby was confident he could do better.

As a result, he committed to creating his own salon—one that would address the weaknesses he saw in the salon industry, foster camaraderie among stylists, and ensure customers had a salon experience worth talking about.

Opportunity Knocks

The year 2008 wasn't exactly the most auspicious time to start a business. The global economy plummeted to a depth not seen since the Great Depression. Across the nation, businesses small and large were imploding at an astonishing pace and the job market was hemorrhaging workers.

One such casualty of the Great Recession was a small salon tucked behind a boutique in an up-and-coming neighborhood in trendy Venice, California. The salon owner had decided to sell the business and wanted out. Upon hearing news of this, Bobby decided to check it out. From the moment he stepped foot into the vacated space, Bobby knew this was the salon he had dreamed of calling his own.

It wasn't lost on Bobby, however, that the nation's economy was in a fragile state and consumers weren't spending freely. Yet despite facing a daunting recession, his own fears and anxieties, and a lack of capital to launch his business, Bobby trusted his gut, took the leap, and became a fledgling entrepreneur.

It required help from those closest to him to make it happen. "I borrowed money from my friends. I traded haircuts for help with the business. In the end, my friends believed in the concept as much as I did and I was able to secure the seed money to get it open," he recalls.

Over the next few months, he poured his heart and soul into establishing his business. Bobby created an intimate space with four salon chairs overlooking a serene garden. The team of skilled stylists he hired was fun and talented and shared his customer service philosophy. The overall vibe of his venture was welcoming and warm, and the haircuts were hip and stylish. And so Hair Venice was born.

Westside LA locals, known for their demand for quality, quickly began buzzing about the salon. Hair Venice took off faster than Bobby could imagine. After all the struggle, sacrifice, and risk, Bobby enjoyed a sense of pride and relief knowing he had finally succeeded in creating the business he had dreamed of.

That is, until he found out about a scathing online review of his business.

Panic Sets In

News of this biting review came from Sally, a longtime loyal customer. During an evening of random web surfing, Sally searched Hair Venice and was led to rating-and-review sites about her beloved salon. They appeared at the top of her search results for Bobby's salon.

Rating-and-Review Sites: These websites permit anyone with an Internet connection to give rating scores to businesses and provide written reviews about their experience. Typical sites in this category include Yelp, TripAdvisor, Angie's List, Citysearch, and many others.

One of the first reviews Sally encountered was particularly nasty. Its biting commentary seemed to describe an antithesis of the Hair Venice experience she had come to know.

At first she didn't think it was necessary to bring it to Bobby's attention. After all, every site falls prey to online trolls. But after some deliberating, Sally became concerned about its potential impact on his business, so she decided to disclose her discovery to Bobby.

As he read the review, each scathing word seemed to morph into 3-D and jump out from the screen. Bobby felt a surge of nausea and dizziness. The post was a one-sided rant filled with hyperbole, insults, and outright lies.

After reading the reviewer's description of events, Bobby immediately recognized her identity.

It was a first-time customer he'd seen a few weeks prior. She had told him on the phone that "no one ever gets my hair right, but I've read great things about you and am hoping you can work a miracle."

At her insistence, Bobby had agreed to squeeze her in toward the end of a long day, though he had other appointments scheduled after her. She was late for her appointment, but Bobby took the time to listen to her concerns and developed a plan to repair some damaged areas of her hair. She agreed to the plan and Bobby worked on her hair. When he was finished, she was not happy with the result, but Bobby had already run over into his next appointment due to her late arrival.

Her demanding demeanor and negative attitude were classic signals of the hard-to-please type—someone who had probably been described as "high maintenance" by the many stylists she'd fired before him.

He offered to see her again in two days to discuss how to address the problems with her haircut and how to set her on the right path.

"Like clockwork," said Boas, "two days later she called and canceled the appointment at the last minute."

Since he had committed to helping her, he agreed, against his better judgment, to reschedule her appointment. She later canceled that appointment, too, this time via text message, and changed her story about what she didn't like about the haircut.

She then posted a lengthy, incoherent, and scathing review on Yelp that at times even contradicted itself. It was horrifying to read, especially when Bobby had worked so hard to address her concerns.

The review baffled him. In it, she made no mention of the extra time and effort he put into her haircut, including the lengthy, free follow-up session he offered. To make matters worse, her negative review appeared at the top of his Hair Venice profile on Yelp.

As the days and weeks passed, the review wouldn't budge from the top of his Yelp profile. Bobby grew increasingly preoccupied by doom-and-gloom scenarios. He wondered:

- How are unfair reviews like this even possible, and do I have a way to defend myself?
- Are there other inaccurate reviews about me on the Internet?
- How many customers have seen this review, and did they believe what they read?
- What if I get more of these from other irrational customers?
- Will reviews like this destroy everything I've worked so hard to create?
- What on earth can I do to fix this?

A New Challenge for Your Business

Statistics show *only half* of new businesses will survive past the five-year mark. And among the half that make it that far, a further two-thirds will close their doors within the first decade. All of which is to say that the entrepreneurial journey rewards the bold, not the meek. In this survival-of-the-fittest marketplace, you know firsthand that success is hard fought, not granted, and you can never let challenges keep you down.

The moment you open your doors, the harsh reality of being a business owner instantly replaces any preconceived fantasies associated with entrepreneurship. Not only do you have to master your own craft, you must also successfully juggle a seemingly endless list of skills that have little or nothing to do with what inspired you to hang your shingle in the first place. Example of these include the following:

- Marketing
- Customer service
- Human resources
- Scheduling
- Accounts payable
- Accounts receivable
- Payroll

One key reason you work hard to fastidiously manage these diverse elements is that they each play an important role in keeping your business running smoothly.

But doing business in the information age has added another significant task to your reputation and brand-building efforts. Rating-and-review sites present unprecedented challenges that directly affect both your online and offline brand and reputation. Even if you master every other skill required to run your business, if you overlook the power of rating-and-review sites, you'll dramatically decrease your competitiveness and your chances of long-term survival.

An Unexpected Call to Action: Why This Feels Unfair

Like Bobby, you may not have realized the power of online ratings and reviews until the eye-opening moment you discovered a damaging post. In a flash, the joy and satisfaction associated with launching your business are replaced with frustration and anxiety.

Like it or not, rating-and-review sites are only growing in size and reach. So whether you're managing your Yelp profile every day or have never opened a web browser in your life, there's no avoiding their influence. Rating-and-review sites are Internet watering holes, virtual agoras where your prospects and clients actively share their thoughts about every aspect of your business.

Even more profoundly, however, potential customers actively seek out this online chatter. It's often their first point of contact for guidance, advice, and recommendations about your business. So their decision to call, email, visit, or pass up your business altogether is dependent on what they learn about you online.

To the uninitiated, however, the rating-and-review platform can feel overwhelmingly complicated and downright intimidating. In fact, throughout my fifteen-year career in public relations and marketing, I've heard a chorus of concerns and complaints from countless business owners. Their frustrations can be summarized in the following three ways:

1. There are too many rating-and-review sites.
You may find yourself asking, "Where should I even start looking for ratings and reviews about my business?" The Internet is a limitless digital space, and the number of rating-and-review sites, as well as the content posted on them, is overwhelming. Unfortunately, small businesses often don't have the resources to fund the staff necessary to identify and monitor these sites.

2. No one asked my permission.
Without your consent, invitation, or knowledge, anyone in the world has the power to post ratings and reviews about your business for all to see. These sites have created sophisticated and elaborate online communities based on businesses like yours—without ever involving you.

3. The system is downright unfair.
If the rating-and-review sites are engaged in a game of playing favorites, the reviewers always seem to win out over the businesses being reviewed. For example, if you disagree with content posted about your business and reach out to the rating-and-review sites for help, the likelihood of their taking action is low. And as consumers increasingly turn to rating-and-review sites as their primary resource, reviewers have greater influence over your business.

In addition, virtually anyone can say anything about you and your business, regardless of whether the comments are true or false.

Businesses Are the Innocent Bystanders

As you may suspect, online rating-and-review sites were created for consumers, *not* you, the business owner. As such, your needs, concerns, and objections were not part of the product design, despite the fact that the entire online ratings and reviews industry exists only because of businesses like yours. Not to mention, a significant source of the industry's revenue comes from business owners who subscribe to paid accounts or advertise on the platforms.

These circumstances have made it possible for you to be harmed, threatened, and manipulated by online rating-and-review sites. I call this being *manipurated* (a combination of the words "manipulated" and "rated").

If you've been manipurated, you understand the importance and clout of online ratings and reviews, and the sour, unsatisfying taste left in your mouth when you realize that owning a successful business puts you in the position of being an unwitting target.

From multinational retail brands to small business owners, anyone can be manipurated. So when it comes to online ratings and reviews, no immunity or hall pass exists for any business. With so much at stake, taking charge of your online ratings and reviews is a must and opting out is not an option.

You Can Fight Back...and Win

Facing the online rating-and-review juggernaut can feel like a modern-day David versus Cyber Goliath. But just as David defeated the giant bully by cleverly using a simple sling and stone, there are practical tools you can use to effectively outsmart your otherwise formidable online adversary.

As with all aspects of running your business, the buck ultimately stops with you. Managing your organization's online ratings and reviews is your responsibility, and yours alone. The good news is business owners, just like you, have actually turned their adversarial relationship with rating-and-review sites into powerful marketing allies that have increased their businesses' revenues.

If you've been manipurated and are uncertain what to do about it, the chapters in Part Two of this book will shed light on effective tactics and strategies you can deploy.

But before we explore these, you first need to establish a solid foundation of understanding—one that will ensure your long-term success.

The next chapter will answer the question "How did we get here?" By understanding the history of this powerful platform, you'll avoid repeating mistakes made by countless business owners before you.

2

The Rise of Ratings and Reviews

In 2012, a frozen yogurt shop in Brooklyn went in search of some Yelp help. The small store had received negative comments on Yelp and other popular rating-and-review sites—a black eye for a fledgling local business. To address the unfavorable reviews as quickly as possible, the store owners planned to hire a reputation management firm. They went about contacting New York's top companies that offered online reputation management services.

When these companies learned about the yogurt shop's online predicament, a few offered a simple solution: populate popular review sites—

In this chapter, you'll learn:

✔ How the rise of the rating-and-review industry is relevant to your strategy

✔ The technical aspects of the rating-and-review industry that have made life challenging for business owners

✔ Why managing your online ratings and reviews must play a crucial role in your overall marketing plan

> **Online Reputation Management:** The practice of shaping public opinion online about a person, business, or issue. Services are offered by consultants and agencies that use technical knowledge to influence what is found on search engines, rating-and-review sites, and other websites.

such as Yelp, Google Local, and Citysearch—with reviews they'd create, distribute, and manage in-house. These positive posts would offset the negative ones and provide the business a much-needed ratings boost, thereby improving its reputation.

Not content with putting their trust in just one of these reputation management companies, the yogurt shop owners decided to hire several firms. After all, the more help the better.

The companies they hired went to work generating positive new reviews. But because the most popular rating-and-review sites have filters and other built-in mechanisms to separate genuine reviews from fake ones, the reputation management firms employed technical wizardry to trick the sites into accepting the new content:

- They used sophisticated methods to hide the identities of those providing fake reviews.
- They established hundreds of online profiles on review sites and used these to post content.
- They had their own employees write reviews.
- They paid freelance writers in faraway locations, such as the Philippines and Bangladesh, to endorse the yogurt shop.

In addition, the reputation management companies used sites such as Craigslist.org, Freelancer.com, and oDesk.com to find more people willing to write reviews for money on the yogurt shop's behalf. One company submitted the following online request:

We need a person that can post multiple positive reviews on major REVIEW sites. Example: Google Maps, Yelp, Citysearch. Must be from different IP addresses... So you must be able to have multiple

IPs. The reviews will be only a few sentences long. Need to have some understanding on how Yelp filters work. Previous experience is a plus...just apply --) we are a marketing company.

By engaging in these slick tactics, little did these companies know they would be caught red-handed in a sophisticated government sting operation.

Across the nation, protecting the public is one of the primary responsibilities of state attorneys general, which is why New York's attorney general, Eric Schneiderman, planned what became known as "Operation Clean Turf." (*Turf* refers to *astroturfing*—the practice of masking fake online reviews in order to make them appear as if they are from legitimate customers.)

The goal of the yearlong undercover crackdown was to hunt down and prosecute companies for false advertising and deceptive business practices, which included astroturfing. Representatives from AG Schneiderman's office posed as the owners of the Brooklyn-based yogurt shop.

In the end, nineteen companies were charged. As part of the settlement, they agreed to stop writing fake online reviews and were fined $350,000 in penalties for flooding the Internet with counterfeit reviews on the country's most popular rating-and-review sites.

In a news release published on his official website, the attorney general said:

> *Consumers rely on reviews from their peers to make daily purchasing decisions on anything from food and clothing to recreation and sightseeing.*

> *This investigation into large-scale, intentional deceit across the Internet tells us that we should approach online reviews with caution. And companies that continue to engage in these practices should take note: "Astroturfing" is the 21st century's version of false advertising, and prosecutors have many tools at their disposal to put an end to it.*

In the same news release, Aaron Schur, Yelp's senior litigation counsel, said, "More than 100 million visitors come to Yelp each month, making it critical that Yelp protect the integrity of its content. . . We applaud NY Attorney General Schneiderman for his willingness to tackle the issue of illegal fake reviews head-on, and for his success in shutting down these operators."

Throughout this book, you'll learn how to effectively manage your online ratings and reviews using legitimate, aboveboard tactics that protect you from the consequences you'd experience by working with an unscrupulous reputation management firm.

While many of these companies promise convenience and quick solutions, hiring them could permanently damage your online reputation.

One thing I've learned over my many years working in digital marketing and technology: specific techniques have a short shelf life. The tips and tricks you read about online to help you manage reviews, and possibly even some of the techniques in this very book, evolve rapidly. Rather than jump straight into tips and techniques, you will benefit from understanding the underlying infrastructure that has made ratings and reviews such a powerful force online.

It's the equivalent of looking at your opposing team's overall strategy rather than its play-by-play performance. Some teams habitually play a long game, using strong offense to wear down their opponents. Others fight with strong and aggressive defense every game.

You can only increase your odds of winning the rating-and-review game in the long run if you embrace the long-game mentality. Otherwise, you'll continually be in defense mode and never feel like you're getting ahead.

It All Started with Search Engines

In the late 1990s, the Internet was still a fledgling consumer technology. Back then if you wanted to find web content, the premier search engine was Yahoo!, which originally stood for Yet Another Hierarchically Organized Oracle.

If you were to peek under the hood and inside Yahoo!'s search engine, you'd see lots of humans staring at computer screens organizing information into lists. Indeed, Yahoo's original structure was designed around human-edited and curated lists of websites on the Internet. It was hand sorted.

This labor-intensive approach could not keep up with the endless stream of websites being built 'round the clock across the globe and waiting to be indexed. By decade's end, performing a Yahoo! search on the information superhighway felt like searching for a grain of rice on the beach.

In 1999, a disruptive force emerged that forever changed the online search experience. That year, Google's two cofounders created a new way to organize Internet search. Rather than relying on manual labor and human-edited lists, they invented a technology that used computer-based algorithms.

Google's computer network retrieved copies of every website it could locate and then stored that content on central servers. Instead of humans, it used networked computers. These computers searched through the compiled information to create the digital equivalent of an old-school library card catalog. When you searched for something on Google, it ran the search query on its computer network and gave you what it felt was the best answer.

Suddenly, the decision-making power of indexing websites shifted from human editors to computers.

And what was the brilliant, almost stupidly simple result?

You'd input a search query on Google.com's now famously clutter-free interface and instantly see a list of highly relevant results. This technology represented a quantum leap when it came to how consumers were able to search for content online. In a sense, the Internet began to organize itself.

Google's algorithm used a variety of criteria to determine where any given site would rank in someone's search results. At the top of its priority list was how many other websites were linking to a particular site. Google's thinking was the site that had the most inbound links (links from other sites) on a particular subject must be a reliable resource for other sites, or hold some kind of topical authority, or both.

For example, when you searched for "best restaurants in San Antonio, Texas," the site with the largest number of other sites linking to it would be ranked highest because it was ostensibly the most relevant.

Although this was a sensible approach, it didn't take long for tech-savvy individuals to figure out that this was how Google ranked sites. Armed with that knowledge, those clever minds developed ways to manipulate Google's search results. Because inbound links were a major factor in indexing a site, these intrepid Internet opportunists created webs of inbound links pointing to a specific page or site.

These tactics became known as link spam and link farms. Most of them were fake—merely pages with lists of links to other pages. With the help of these cyber schemes, the likelihood of a page or site faking its way to the top search results became predictably high and could be sustained by continuing to create even more links.

Crafty tactics such as these signaled the birth of a new electronic industry: Search Engine Optimization (SEO). Once SEO's subversive origins were exposed, companies—from mom-and-pop to Fortune 500—embraced it. Its use grew exponentially and developed into a mega-industry. In fact, in 2014 alone, companies invested an estimated $4 billion in their SEO efforts.[1]

Enter the Fresh Factor

During my time at Google, early in my career, I met some of high tech's smartest engineers. Among Google's best and brightest were those tasked with beating back Internet opportunists trying to trick the company's algorithm, finding bulletproof ways to verify which sites had bona fide authority on a search topic. This was no easy task, and it challenged the fundamental structure of Google's entire approach to search.

These Google engineers were always launching tests, trying to find ways to neutralize the black hat SEO tactics. They quickly discovered how easily SEO companies could manipulate inbound

---

1 www.seoaudit.com/key-seo-advertising-trends.php

SEO: Black Versus White

The SEO (Search Engine Optimization) industry is built on companies and consultants whose goal is to help their clients' sites show up more frequently and higher on a list of search results. As with any large industry, you'll find companies and consultants who engage in ethical and unethical practices.

Legitimate SEO tactics are known as **white hat SEO**. They include properly selecting keywords on a site and optimizing site pages for mobile platforms.

On the other hand, there's **black hat SEO**. This is SEO's dark side. It refers to manipulative techniques that fake it to try to make it. Black hat tactics, such as link spam, are designed to subvert search engine algorithms to falsely boost a site's search ranking.

links to their advantage. Although Google engineers continued to use inbound links to evaluate a website's quality, their exhaustive research uncovered a promising new concept.

That concept is now known as *freshness*, which is the frequency with which a particular page is updated with new content.

Ultimately, Google determined that a search result based on both inbound links *and* freshness was better than one that considered just inbound links alone.

As a result, Google changed its algorithm to pay attention to both. By adding freshness, Google did not know it also changed the rules of the SEO game.

Today, sites that continually receive new content or whose content is frequently updated are considered fresh. And in Google's eyes, fresher is better.

Freshness and Yelp's Ascent

As far as your business is concerned, 2005 was a big year—even if your company did not exist then. That year marked the launch of a new start-up called Yelp.

Before Yelp, consumers would search for businesses and read reviews from professional reviewers or critics, or they would ask friends and family for recommendations. It was hard to find out what other people outside their circle of friends and family had to say about a particular business.

Yelp solved that problem with its consumer-driven rating-and-review platform, allowing anyone with an Internet connection to rate and review a business. It also allowed everyone to see that feedback. It was a collective electronic journal that chronicled multiple consumer experiences for the entire world to see, unedited and unfiltered.

This focus on generating massive amounts of new content every single day put Yelp right in Google's freshness sweet spot. It was the equivalent of an information salad bar in the middle of a convenience store full of junk food information.

The convergence between Yelp's freshness and inbound links and the preference Google placed on both created a windfall for Yelp. The company burst onto the search result scene, with its ratings and reviews taking center stage on the world's biggest search engine. Yelp's ratings and reviews soon launched to the top search results of most local business categories. Today, if you search Google for something like "best sushi in Dallas," within the first few search results you'll find a Yelp rating and review.

And dozens of other popular rating-and-review sites leveraged Google's algorithm and experienced similarly successful search engine results. Many of them address specific business categories, such as law, medicine, and home repair:

- **Avvo**—a lawyer rating-and-review site
- **Healthgrades**—a physician rating-and-review site
- **Angie's List**—a paid subscription site that provides information about many different kinds of service providers, such as plumbers, gardeners, and doctors

Yet as popular as these other companies are, Yelp reigns supreme. It has more than 130 million monthly visitors. For that reason, it's often also seen as a kingmaker for businesses. Do well on Yelp, it's believed, and you do well in business.

Yelp Profile: Growing Pains of an Evolving Platform

Yelp is the undisputed market leader in online rating-and-review sites. Its high profile also means it receives the lion's share of negative publicity.

To be fair, all rating-and-review sites have flaws. At the same time, complaints about Yelp seem pervasive enough to have compelled the company to dedicate part of its website to addressing them.

Many of Yelp's critics find fault with the company's rating-and-review strategy, which sets it apart from other similar sites.

Why Yelp Hides Some Reviews and Promotes Others

When it comes to rating-and-review sites, a question I'm often asked is "Why do old, outdated ratings and reviews consistently remain at the top, while recent ones are either given low priority or hidden from view altogether?" And those asking me are usually referring to a negative rating and review that maintains a doggedly high profile.

By default, most rating-and-review sites order content by **recency**. This means content appears chronologically, from most recent to oldest. Yelp's algorithm, on the other hand, uses other factors in addition to recency, which it argues lends credibility to its ratings and reviews.

Part of Yelp's emphasis includes prioritizing reviews based on the reviewer's identity. Yelp knows a lot about the reviewers who are frequently active on its platform. But it does not know much about reviewers who infrequently use the service or rarely write reviews. It is a social hierarchy, of course, consisting of Yelp's most active reviewers at the top and its least active reviewers at the bottom.

At the very top of the social structure lives Yelp's aristocracy—they are part of an invite-only program. This is the category with the fewest number of people. Called the Yelp Elite Squad, these select reviewers comprise Yelp's most favored contributors.

The controversial Yelp Elite Squad program allows businesses to buy access to Yelp Elite Squad members for special events, all in hopes of soliciting strong reviews and thus visibility. Consumer watchdogs have called on Yelp to modify or abandon this program altogether because they assert it creates a conflict of interest.

Yelp contends its strategy promotes reviewers who have an established history on the platform (particularly those with Yelp Elite Squad status). This increases the authenticity of the company's ratings and reviews.

However, anyone with persistence and creativity can easily manipulate Yelp's platform. No doubt, for every move Yelp makes to improve its algorithm, countless countermoves emerge that undermine Yelp's efforts. This creates problems for businesses and consumers who rely on the site for reliable content.

Overall, Yelp's system can be maddeningly imperfect. Its flaws make it ripe for industry experts to easily manipulate it.

The Role of Consumer Online Search Behavior

Because rating-and-review sites are loaded with Google-pleasing fresh content, when people search for your business, they're almost guaranteed to see rating-and-review sites at the top of their results. In fact, you may be shocked to discover that these sites actually outrank your own website in the search results.

This begs the question "So how does this affect my business?"

The answer to the question lies with consumer search behavior, and what I'm about to share may disappoint you.

Research has proved more than half of consumers do not search beyond the first page of results.[2] Furthermore, they are most likely to click on the very first search result.

In this scenario, search results in second place and below are about as effective as having no presence at all. Therefore, if a rating-and-review site is the first result in a search about your business, then your prospects are most likely bypassing your site completely.

Consumers aren't finding you. Rather, they're finding your Yelp profile and its version of you.

Research has shown that consumers also trust what they read online, compounding that disposition toward laziness.[3]

Think about the conundrum: if a rating-and-review site is the first search result about your business, and the content on that site is the main way people are learning about you, these sites are robbing you of the opportunity to influence their perception of your business.

Star Power: The Importance of Ratings

For a business owner, finding cringe-worthy reviews about you on a rating-and-review site is never fun. After all, you're not getting up at 6:00 a.m. every morning to build a two-star business bogged down by negative reviews.

---

2 www.searchenginejournal.com/24-eye-popping-seo-statistics/42665
3 searchengineland.com/88-consumers-trust-online-reviews-much-personal-recommendations-195803

But damaged egos alone aren't the only reason you should be concerned with negative ratings and reviews and focused on cultivating positive ones. They translate to literal dollars that affect your bottom line.

When it comes to ratings in particular, studies from both Harvard University and the University of California, Berkeley, have shown a direct link between star ratings and revenue. For most companies, a seemingly minor one-star boost can result in a 10 percent increase in business. For restaurants, the impact is even more significant. An uptick from three and a half to four stars can lead to a 19 percent increase in peak-hour bookings.[4, 5]

Manipurated: The Emergence of Manipulating Ratings and Reviews

As the rating-and-review sites have skyrocketed in popularity, so have their influence on consumer behavior. People across the globe are turning to these sites in droves, believing what they read and making purchase decisions that bypass business owners entirely.

The New York attorney general's yogurt shop sting was just one example among countless others that illustrate the widespread and harmful fraud in the rating-and-review industry.

Like flies to a turd, it's no surprise that these sites have drawn the interest of online opportunists keen on pursuing their own agenda and interests.

This maelstrom also draws in vengeful customers, unscrupulous competitors, and SEO companies that corrupt the platforms themselves. Sadly, businesses such as yours are squarely in the bull's-eye.

---

4 www.hbs.edu/faculty/Publication%20Files/12-016_0464f20e-35b2-492e-a328-fb14a325f718.pdf
5 news.berkeley.edu/2012/09/04/yelp-reviews-boost-restaurant-business/

Regulators Struggle to Rein In Fake Reviews

Government watchdogs have been grappling with the challenges of regulating the mercurial rating-and-review industry. Their efforts have mainly focused on one of the most pervasive issues: fake reviews.

As you'll see in upcoming chapters, fake reviews represent a fundamental challenge for the rating-and-review industry and your business. A Harvard study compiled more than 300,000 Yelp reviews and found, from 2006 to 2014, fake reviews skyrocketed from six percent to twenty percent.[6] Yelp itself disclosed that approximately 25 percent of the reviews it receives are fake.

In 2009, the Federal Trade Commission (FTC) published its report for businesses governing online endorsements and testimonials. The FTC's initial recommendations dealt primarily with hired spokespeople and celebrity endorsements across the Internet, but the FTC later added amendments that specifically addressed fake online reviews.

The following year, the FTC successfully settled charges against Reverb Communications, a public relations agency. The FTC accused the company of actively writing reviews on the Apple iTunes store for a game-developer client without disclosing its relationship with the game-developer itself.

Part of the settlement required the PR agency to remove the reviews without having to admit to any wrongdoing. This example points to how online rating-and-review malfeasance most of the time receives mere slap-on-the-wrist punishments, if any at all.

---

6 people.hbs.edu/mluca/FakeItTillYouMakeIt.pdf

3

The Business of Cyberbullying

• •

"I'm the only person over 40 who does not want to be 22 again," said Monica Lewinsky, during her 2015 presentation to a group attending the well-known TED conference.

In 1998, when news of her affair with President Bill Clinton broke, the recent college graduate and White House staff member instantly became one of the most infamous and widely recognized women in the world.

Before the Oval Office sex scandal, major news stories spread through the three traditional media channels: TV, print, and radio.

In this chapter, you'll learn:

✔ How being manipurated is part of a larger social trend toward aggressive and hateful speech online

✔ How competing interests create an inherent conflict of interest for rating-and-review sites

✔ How the industry should self-regulate to better protect itself, consumers, and businesses

News of Lewinsky's, shall we say, "involvement" with the commander in chief exposed a new phenomenon. It was one of the initial instances of major news exploding around the world via the Internet, which at that time was still in its dial-up stage of development. Thanks to the burgeoning digital revolution, the story broadcast around the world at unprecedented speed.

To make matters worse for the twenty-two-year-old, throughout the affair she had confided in Linda Tripp, a fellow White House employee. Although Lewinsky didn't know it at the time, Tripp had recorded their private conversations in which Lewinsky had gone into great detail about her romance with the president.

Twenty hours of intimate conversations eventually made their way online—Lewinsky's words as a young adult became a permanent part of the national archive, thanks to the Internet.

As part of the investigation, Lewinsky had to authenticate the recordings. She described how it felt to hear her own words:

> *Scared and mortified, I listen, listen as I prattle on about the flotsam and jetsam of the day; listen as I confess my love for the president, and, of course, my heartbreak; listen to my sometimes catty, sometimes churlish, sometimes silly self being cruel, unforgiving, uncouth; listen, deeply, deeply ashamed, to the worst version of myself, a self I don't even recognize.*

No sooner than you can say "information superhighway," Monica Lewinsky went from being a private citizen to the target of ridicule, much of it online.

The loss of dignity, her indelibly tarnished reputation, and the humiliation she experienced through what she described as "mobs of virtual stone throwers" led to depression and thoughts of suicide.

"I was branded as a tramp, tart, slut, whore, bimbo, and, of course, that woman. I was seen by many but actually known by few," she said.

At the time, her online shaming had no name. Today we call it cyberbullying. In this chapter, we'll explore what cyberbullying is and how it applies to your online ratings and reviews.

Welcome to a Notorious Club

If you've been a victim of hate-laced reviews or some form of written attack from unknown online parties, you know what it's like to be cyberbullied.

It's a global crisis—an outgrowth of the information age that has affected business owners and private citizens around the world. As Lewinsky described it, web-based humiliation is a dehumanizing experience that can have long-lasting repercussions.

Cyberbullying is so complicated, pervasive, and unprecedented that even the courts have struggled to define a legal framework to deal with it.

One area that's making some progress is the public education sector. Public schools across the country have established disciplinary guidelines regarding cyberbullying. However, within the private commercial sector, which includes the rating-and-review sites, little has been done to address the issue.

When you are cyberbullied on rating-and-review sites, I believe the sites themselves should provide clear measures to protect you, the victim. In order to establish an effective set of protocols, all rating-and-review stakeholders would need to cooperate: the sites themselves, the people who post content, and you.

Unfortunately, the rating-and-review system lacks accountability, transparency, and integrity. I'm continually baffled that most rating-and-review sites take a passive approach to addressing the issue.

There are two sides to a cyberbullying communication: the speech itself (meaning the actual words) and the recipient or target of the speech. Most sites on the Internet have argued in favor of, and built their systems around, protecting the speech. They have done very little to protect the target of the speech.

Conflicts of Interest Put Business Owners at Risk

The online rating-and-review industry is a multibillion-dollar web-based giant. And it hasn't reached its commercial heights through altruism or good deeds. Make no mistake—these sites are businesses that exist to generate profit.

Their revenue model relies on a crushing flow of new ratings and reviews, and any attempt to restrict the flow of that content would put their ability to rank highly on Google in jeopardy. That's bad for business.

This creates a conflict of interest: Any gesture rating-and-review sites make to withhold or restrict content could dramatically decrease their web traffic. And lower web traffic means lower revenues. This may explain why their digital police force does such a lousy job removing content that lacks credibility.

How Rating-and-Review Sites Take Action

The conflicts of interest make it difficult for the rating-and-review sites to effectively tackle common complaints from business owners. The following are three of the industry's fundamental flaws and how different rating-and-review sites are addressing them:

1. Weak Reviewer Verification: Addressing an Identity Crisis

Rating-and-review sites all struggle with the right approach to validating the reviews that they publish or host. Yelp contends that its algorithm, which favors reviews from its most active members, acts as a check-and-balance.

But look at things from the perspective of those writing the review. Unlike a food critic at a large magazine, or a journalist covering a new product, reviewers on a rating-and-review site are not bound by a code of ethics. Indeed, they may be in it purely for personal satisfaction, and from their perspective, the pressure's on to create reviews that get lots of attention. This is often achieved by embellishing reviews with over-the-top words and hyperbole. Collectively, those rants, half-truths, and occasionally absurd commentary may seem more suited for a blog titled *Digital Diary of a Manic Depressive*.

As a business owner it may seem like you're riding on a bipolar roller coaster. One day, it's a glowing description:

The best service EVER! I'm a customer for life!

Meanwhile, the next day:

> *Who would EVER recommend this place?*
> *NEVER again!*

Or perhaps both appear on the *same* day.

If reviewers were honest 100 percent of the time, most of their comments would appear more informative and factual, and less hyperbolic. As a result, the problems associated with egregious and inaccurate reviews would probably cease to exist. But in the rating-and-review popularity contest, the most outrageous voices often receive the most attention.

One way to promote honesty is to increase accountability.

Identity Verification

Unfortunately, checks and balances that would boost the credibility of ratings and reviews are nearly nonexistent, and most sites fight them on the grounds that they would "chill" or restrain free speech. They argue that, on the Internet, consumers have a right to be anonymous.

In addition, developing solutions to confront this dilemma would require the rating-and-review sites to first admit they're facing an existential crisis.

Amazon, for its part, has attempted to raise reviewer accountability with its Verified Purchase mark. When a rating and review comes from a customer who actually purchased a product on Amazon, the company designates the rating and review as a Verified Purchase. The customer can choose to write under any pseudonym he or she would like and has the privilege of doing so anonymously. But at least the reader knows an actual product changed hands. As you'll see in the next chapter, even this approach is not without its challenges.

In another example, TripAdvisor and American Express teamed to launch an opt-in review-verification program. Consumers who hold American Express cards and have a TripAdvisor account can connect the two systems via American Express.

When those American Express customers have a hotel charge on their statements, American Express invites them to post a rating and review on TripAdvisor. The rating and review is marked with an icon that indicates it is based on a customer's actual hotel stay.

While Amazon and TripAdvisor still post ratings and reviews that come from other nonverified origins, the companies are at least attempting to increase reviewer accountability by ensuring some transaction took place. By verifying those ratings and reviews, they also raise the trustworthiness of that content.

In an ideal world, Yelp would also move to implement a similar system of accountability. The company could create an infrastructure—say, via one-time redemption codes on a receipt that get entered into Yelp—that would prove that reviewers actually have had an experience with the service they're rating and reviewing.

2. Business Owner Grievance Process

In my research for this book, I spoke with multiple business owners whose complaints regarding rating-and-review sites were variations on the following theme:

I come under attack from customers who have never used my business. They're frauds.

In some instances, business owners believed their competitors were using rating-and-review sites to actually target them. And when misconduct took place, requests that rating-and-review sites take action were ignored. In general, business owners expressed feelings of powerlessness.

Some business owners have used the courts to force the rating-and-review sites to address inaccurate or fake content. Many lawsuits involved attempts to force a site to unmask a reviewer's identity. Thus far, the courts have generally ruled in favor of consumers rather than businesses on the grounds of not limiting free speech.

3. Lack of Algorithm Transparency

When I worked at Google, reporters frequently asked me how the world's most popular search engine went about identifying the rank and order of its search results. In particular, how did Google determine what sites were worthy of the sacred number one search result spot?

One of the main reasons Google avoids disclosing its ranking criteria is that it would enable the fraudsters and hacks whose goal is to use the information to their benefit.

Similarly, rating-and-review sites are overwhelmingly terrible at disclosing—to business owners, regulators, consumers, God, and everyone else—the methodology their proprietary software uses to reach decisions on the ranking and order of ratings and reviews on their sites.

When pressed for answers, the rating-and-review sites frequently describe the benefits of editorial neutrality. In other words, secret algorithms increase objectivity and accuracy in terms of what content appears on their sites and how it should be ordered and displayed.

But insider experience has taught me that regardless of how inherently objective an algorithm is, at one point a human wrote it. And humans most likely continue to train and fine-tune it as well.

Rating-and-review sites owe business owners more disclosure about how they make decisions—whether human generated or computer generated or a combination of the two.

Some sites avoid problems associated with secret algorithms by keeping their formula simple. They rank ratings and reviews in the order they were received. Yelp does not do this, and as you've read, their approach is a big part of the problem with their system. I believe complaints about Yelp are warranted and it's time for the company to address business owners' concerns.

But if past behavior is the most accurate predictor of future behavior, Yelp is unlikely to disclose key information about its algorithm anytime soon.

The Internet Behaving Badly

Cyberbullying within the rating-and-review sites is part of a larger crisis within the Internet. Anyone with a profile on any number of platforms is subject to it. And innocent victims have little to no recourse to stop perpetrators from continuing their online abuse.

Some online rating-and-review companies have taken some action to combat cyberbullying. They have increased accountability by adding verification protocols or have made access more difficult by adding certain membership thresholds. But considering how popular, well funded, and sophisticated the industry has become, any efforts are insufficient and, for the most part, continue to allow the free flow of inaccurate and fraudulent content.

The refusal of the rating-and-review industry to take decisive and organized action against cyberbullying has created a litany of problems that are detailed in the next chapter.

4

Manipurated:
Where It Went Wrong

Lost Utopia

In an ideal world, the rating-and-review sites would benefit business owners and consumers equally: Business owners would have direct feedback about their products and services, allowing them to identify strengths and weaknesses and continually improve their business model. And consumers would make better decisions armed with accurate, trustworthy content.

We're not in that idyllic Utopian universe, at least not yet. The industry has fundamental problems it must address, and not all of them are the fault of the rating-and-review sites.

In this chapter, you'll learn:

✔ What fake ratings and reviews are and how they harm your business

✔ Techniques to spot fake reviews

✔ What paid services are offered by rating-and-review sites

✔ The role reputation management companies play in your online rating-and-review strategy

This chapter reveals the players manipulating online ratings and reviews, the inner workings of how they exploit the platforms to their benefit, and, ultimately, how your business is left cleaning up the mess. Specifically, you'll learn three ways your business is targeted by these shady characters.

1. Works of Fiction: Fake Reviews

Tina is a recent college graduate who lives in the sunny, seaside town of San Diego, California. She's self-employed, works from home, and runs a successful business—a dream scenario for many. The intelligent and intrepid entrepreneur earns her living writing online reviews, with a niche focusing on beauty, skin, and hair care products.

Tina spends up to eight hours a day conducting research and composing creative, well-written reviews. In fact, she prides herself on her writing process, which involves a thorough analysis, addressing questions her readers will most likely ask, and accurate product information.

But there's a dark twist to Tina's business model: what she writes is fictional. While most of her online audience believes her reviews are unbiased and free of conflicts of interest, the truth is, the beauty, skin, and hair care manufacturers themselves actually pay her to write reviews.

She has developed technical expertise that tricks Amazon, Yelp, and Google into thinking her reviews are authentic. Tina knows how to mask her computer's IP address in order for her reviews to appear as if they are generated from different locations. She painstakingly keeps track of her multiple profiles to stay below the radar of rating-and-review sites. And her fastidious efforts protect her clients' interests and result in high-profile reviews.

Tina's even found ways to bypass verification protocols on review sites such as Amazon's Verified Purchase program, which you learned about on page 28. When a review is labeled with the Verified Purchase mark, Amazon assures readers that the author of the review has actually purchased the product on its site. When a company hires Tina to post a Verified review, she purchases the product herself and is reimbursed by her client (in other words, the company who hired her to write the review).

She then composes a review that meets her high copywriting standards. In the end, it receives the Amazon Verified Purchase stamp of approval, isn't stuffed with amateurish keywords that would immediately flag it as phony, and appears 100 percent legitimate.

So how would Amazon customers know the difference between Tina's fake review and a real one? The answer is they probably wouldn't, even if she never opened the package containing the product she purchased.

She's so good at manipulating the rating-and-review sites that at one point, she ranked as one of Yelp's most active reviewers, which means her technical trickery advanced to the stage that even the world's smartest engineers and complex algorithms can't separate her phony reviews from the legitimate ones.

Like many great (and subversive) authors, Tina writes under pseudonyms that protect her real identity and allow her to create personalities that better align with the products she's reviewing or prospective consumers or both. On Google alone, she has over six accounts.

In my interviews with her, I was amazed at her intricate approach, which seemed more like that of a Hollywood method actor than a fake online reviewer. Her process begins by developing her reviewer persona through formulating a story and a character.

"Sometimes the characters are true to life—borrowed from my own opinions and life experiences," Tina says. "I often change my gender, age range, and marital status based upon the type of product or business, and my perceived concept of what a customer for that product or service looks like."

She also highlights the product features that consumers should pay attention to. Tina writes about why she wanted the product, and the information aligns with the needs of potential consumers. Her reviews have one goal in mind: to be identified as the best for a given product listing. "I get a lot of return business that way," she says.

In order for her reviews to be accepted as the real thing, she often includes a fake name linked to her real photo.

"My photograph, if reverse-image searched on Google, would pull up associations with close to a dozen random names. In retrospect, this makes me feel a little strange," she says.

As a business owner who's been manipurated, you may look at someone like Tina and think she lacks a moral or ethical compass. I asked her this question. She described her own code of ethics, which has led her to pass up certain assignments.

"I've been asked to write reviews for child care services, which gave me a horrible feeling," she says.

The assignment to write a review for a day care–preschool facility posed an ethical dilemma as well as a legal one. She feared she could be putting children at risk and give parents a false sense of security about their child's care. And she definitely didn't want to be held responsible for the review itself. This is where she drew the line.

In general, Tina believes her contributions are for the overall good of the industry. And other fake review writers I spoke with shared a similar sentiment.

"I look at it this way," Tina says. "If this company has positive reviews, they are being held to a higher standard. It's up to them to rise to the occasion and keep their reputation good. My one review isn't going to make or break a business or customer."

If you've been manipurated, I doubt you would agree with her benign attitude. Unfortunately, Tina is just one example of the rating-and-review industry's most glaring and prevalent problem—fake reviews.

Defining Fake Ratings and Reviews: Blurred Lines

Many fake ratings and reviews will immediately fail the "sniff test" and provide many readers an intuitive feeling that raises suspicions about a particular rating or review's authenticity or accuracy. But others, such as Tina's, are tougher to identify, even when her reviews are works of fiction.

Another version of this type of review portrays an actual interaction but falsely represents the actual experience the reviewer had with the product or service.

This was the case of the reviewer known as Dan W., who posted one-star ratings and reviews on Yelp about a restaurant located in Millbrae, California. In his reviews, he complained that the restaurant refused to seat him because he was alone and hadn't met the business's dress code standards.

What Dan W. didn't know was that the restaurant had closed-circuit television cameras that recorded his entering the restaurant and leaving in twenty-two seconds without ever interacting with restaurant staff. The restaurant went public with this information and debunked his phony negative experience with the truth—BUSTED!

While Dan W.'s example is provocative and empowering to business owners, most of you won't have audiovisual evidence to prove a rating or review is fake.

Many of the reviews that will vex you fall into more of a gray zone. As was the case with Bobby and his Hair Venice salon, sometimes reviewers present an unbalanced account of their experience.

These reviews fail to document both sides of the story. They often exaggerate unflattering aspects of an encounter, leave out complimentary and positive aspects, and incorporate some degree of creative license, to put it mildly. They're distorted, one sided, and unfair, but it can be argued that they're not *technically* fake.

Spotting Fake Reviews

Although some fake reviews are more difficult to detect than others, with enough practice you'll be able to find the many counterfeit ones. The following are signs to look for:

1. Balanced reviewer profile

Examine the author's other reviews, if you can find them. Can you identify patterns in his or her star ratings? Does this person write the same type of review for a large number of businesses, often saying the same thing? Does the reviewer ever point out a criticism or make a suggestion for improvement? Your answers to these questions will help you determine legitimate content from fake content. Also, a poorly written reviewer profile is a sign that the ratings and reviews coming from this profile are phony.

2. Reviewer's location

Pay attention to the place of origin of the ratings and reviews. Let's say you're looking at ratings and reviews of a hair salon in Austin, Texas. You'd logically assume that many of the reviewers would be locals—people who live nearby and frequent the salon. So why are you seeing amazing, glowing five-star reviews from a suspicious reviewer who lists his or her home city as Zagreb, Croatia? Sure, this could be a legitimate rating and review. But chances are, it isn't.

3. Gaps in review dates

When you look at ratings and reviews for a business, do you find wide gaps in posting dates, with a large group of reviews written in a very small period of time? Does it appear the business gets many reviews at once, or are the reviews posted more or less on a consistent basis? Most businesses will find reviews spread out over a period of time. If you notice that a competitor has groups of very positive reviews all written in a small period of time, you might be looking at some fake reviews.

4. Truth versus fiction

You probably know your competitor's business well. For instance, let's say many of your customers have complained about the terrible parking at your competitor's location. Do any of these complaints appear on your competitor's rating-and-review profile? Do you see reviews that appear to counter those criticisms? Using the parking example, you might see reviews like "Unlike other reviewers, I thought parking was so easy! Convenient and A++." While this cheery remark does not guarantee the review is fake, it certainly should raise suspicion.

5. Contrived and odd reviews
Does the review appear too short, contrived, or lacking detail? Research has shown fake reviews use shorter words than real reviews. A review in this category might say, "most amazing experience, definitely worth coming back! I cannot wait for the next time," while avoiding sharing any real details about the business or the experience.

If I find a fake review, what can I do?
If you suspect a rating and review may be phony, I recommend you flag it with the rating-and-review site. You'll find further information about flagging reviews in Chapter 11. Unfortunately, convincing the rating-and-review site to do anything about it is an uphill battle. At the same time, if the site chooses to take action you'll have solved the immediate problem, so it's worth the small effort.

2. Pay to Play: Rating-and-Review Sites

If you've been in business for any period of time, you've probably experienced the joy of solicitation calls from rating-and-review sites wanting your money. As a business owner myself I receive cold calls like these all the time, and I don't even have a physical storefront.

When rating-and-review sites call, they're usually pitching advertising opportunities, more prominent listings of your business on their sites, improved or featured rankings on their site, and even help with managing problematic ratings and reviews.

While these services are appealing, they do come at a price. In the world of online ratings and reviews, it's a pay-to-play environment, which leads us to yet another way your business is manipurated: these sites generate significant revenue through paid subscriptions and premier services they offer you.

How Small Businesses Foot the Bill

If I were a rating-and-review site apologist, I would argue these sites have earned the right to ask for your money. After all, they've built hugely successful sites used by millions of people all over the world. In fact, rating-and-review site sales reps often tout the unrivaled marketing opportunities their global platform provides business owners. It's not untrue, even if it doesn't always sit well with me.

First, these sites were built for consumers, not the businesses they profile. They were intended to be a forum for information sharing between consumers to help them make better decisions about where to eat, shop, and procure services.

In other words, their target audience is consumers who post content about your business, and other consumers who find and research that content. These sites were not created for the small businesses that form the backbone of what's being discussed on the sites themselves.

Next, the rating-and-review sites were built to make money. To achieve this, they are built at their core as advertising companies. In order to continually increase market share, they're constantly finding new ways to motivate people to read and write about your business. Like a magazine or newspaper, they generate a significant amount of revenue from selling access to that audience.

This paradox is what irritates you: they're hosting a giant virtual town hall about your business for free, giving an open mic to anyone who has an opinion, and then turning around and selling you access to attend.

In other words, it feels like this: "Hey, look pal! We've assembled this large group of people gossiping about your business, sharing their stories about your business, and talking about you. You probably need to be here, but unless you pay me I will only let you stand in the back of the room and listen. It's probably going to go poorly for you. Pay up!"

Buyer's Remorse

Getting back to the issue of cold calls—which all business owners receive—the promises of a bright future routinely delivered by sales reps will one day inevitably catch you at the very moment you are staring at a damning rating or review from an unhappy customer (fake or real). You'll probably be feeling helpless and in desperate need to find a fast solution to your online predicament.

Unfortunately, rating-and-review service companies have earned a reputation for over-promising and under-delivering. You may never experience the benefits you anticipated. Even worse, the terrible rating and review that motivated you to pay for services in the first place may remain firmly planted at the top of your online profile. Meanwhile, a long list of positive reviews may remain buried at the bottom of your profile and even marked "not recommended" by the platform's algorithm.

Is It Online Extortion?

Many small business owners have told me about less-than-friendly solicitation calls from rating-and-review sites. One scenario experienced by many businesses goes like this:

> A Yelp sales rep calls and warns that if you refuse to pay for a business listing on Yelp's site, it will mean your competitors will be able to place their ads on your Yelp profile. On the other hand, if you pay Yelp, your competitors' ads will magically go away.

Sounds downright fraudulent, doesn't it? It might seem similar to shady accounts of the unfriendly neighborhood thug who pledged *not* to take a baseball bat to a shopkeeper's storefront—as long as she paid him protection money. No doubt, in some parts of the world such practices are part of *omertà*—the code of silence associated with organized crime.

In marketing speak, the Yelp example would be categorized as *fear-based selling,* which means using the dread of experiencing dire consequences to convince a prospective buyer into signing up and forking over money for a particular product or service. Meanwhile, most rating-and-review sites would likely argue that stirring up fear in small businesses is not their intent. But most business owners I've met would strongly disagree.

Give Me the One-Star Review!
How One Small Business Battled Yelp

When you ask Davide Cerretini, proprietor of Botto Bistro, what his goal is for Yelp reviews, his answer may surprise you. "I want to be the worst Italian restaurant on the site,"

The Richmond, California, restaurateur has successfully lobbied satisfied customers to write snarky one-star Yelp reviews.

My food arrived before I wanted it to come.

It was too hot to eat.

It brought back all kinds of terrible memories of eating in Italy.

The reason behind the one-star campaign? Cerretini believed Yelp was manipulating ratings and reviews to benefit its best advertisers—a charge Yelp vehemently denies.

His restaurant has even devoted a page on its website to its "Hate Us on Yelp" campaign:

It takes great chefs, great talent and great experience to get a Michelin star, but to get a one-star score on Yelp it takes way more.

You need balls, bad attitude (Italian if possible), the media and the support of the public.

In other words, you need a revolution.

That is exactly what we had, a revolution. Thousands of responses, e-mails and, most importantly, over 2000 one-star reviews written with sarcasm by Botto supporters from all over the country and also overseas. Quite a result for the greatest "vaffanculo" in Yelp history.

We promised to our loyal customers that we were going to be the worst restaurant on Yelp, and here you have it.

We never doubted for a moment that the American public would give us such important support.

In fact, this amazing reward is the result of what people can do together.

This Yelp One-star is all yours, dear friends.

Thank you to all the thousands of fans who wrote these incredibly funny reviews—we really hope they won't be lost in a useless Yelp file of "removed reviews," they were too funny.

At one point, Davide offered customers a 25 percent dining discount for writing a one-star review, but when Yelp discovered Davide's reward program, it sent him an email citing "complaints from the community that you may be offering incentives in exchange for reviews."

Davide's experience is a reminder that despite all the concerns with Yelp and other rating-and-review sites, your most important relationship is still with your customer. As long as you consistently provide a great product or service that your customers are excited about, you might find yourself pleasantly surprised they'll go to battle to protect your good name.

3. Guns for Hire:
Reputation Management Companies

The rating-and-review industry has given rise to a whole new cottage industry of unscrupulous profit seekers who use the industry's technical complexity to extract revenue from your pocketbook.

You previously learned that reputation management involves shaping public opinion online about a person, business, or issue. Reputation management is offered as a service by consultants and agencies that use technical knowledge to influence what is found on search engines, rating-and-review sites, and other websites.

There are legitimate reputation management companies in the industry that offer worthwhile services. There are also companies in this part of the industry that inhabit the darkest, most evil corners of the Internet. Their technical expertise makes them potentially very dangerous to your business.

The following are three reputation management groups you should avoid at all costs. These consultants and companies profit by exploiting weaknesses in the rating-and-review industry:

- Scam artists
- Price gougers
- Disappearing acts

Scam Artists

In 2015, news spread within the professional photography community of a sophisticated scam that was targeting photographers. It had three distinct steps.

First step: A photographer receives an email inquiry from a prospective client asking general questions about the photographer's business. Unbeknownst to the photographer, this email's real purpose is to verify the business's existence. By replying with the requested information, the photographer confirms to the perpetrator that his or her business is legitimate and real.

Second step: Days later, the photographer receives another email message claiming to be a "private investigator [PI] and forensic IT investigator." The email warns that photographers have recently

43

been targeted with fake, harmful ratings and reviews from their competitors. If he or she were to be a victim of this, the private investigator promises to help remove the reviews in an expedited fashion and boasts of a 100 percent success rate.

Third step: About a week later, the photographer receives a third email, this time from a different email address. The email threatens the photographer with "scathing reviews about your business." If the scam goes as planned, the third email will prompt the photographer to contact the PI in the second email.

Most of the photographers who reached out to the PI for help failed to notice one glaring glitch: The first two emails inquiring about their businesses and offering to provide private investigation services came from the same email address. Only the third email that threatened to post fake, damaging reviews was sent from a different one.

This extortion scheme is pure blackmail and is only one example among many of the online entities lurking in the Internet's shadows. Through my work, I've encountered many small business owners across a wide range of industries who have fallen prey to similar scams.

Sinister consultants and organizations will stop at nothing to exploit the rating-and-review system, which means they often target you, the business owner. They leverage the Achilles' heel of most rating-and-review sites—the fact that anyone can write a review anonymously, without any verification that their experience is legitimate.

They also know the visceral and legitimate fears business owners have regarding negative ratings and reviews. Like electronic vultures, they prey on the misfortunes of business owners who have found themselves the recipients of negative reviews.

Even if most people they target ignore their scams, their vile business model requires only a handful of unknowing victims to sign up for their services. If you're one of the lucky ones who hasn't been exposed to reputation management scams yet, by learning from the mistakes of other small business owners you'll protect yourself from making grave errors that could be both costly and difficult, if not impossible, to resolve.

Price Gougers

Service providers within this category are called *price gougers* because they are severely overpriced, using techniques and tactics that most of you can accomplish at very little cost on your own. Many of these service providers charge between $3,000 and $15,000 *per month* for their services. That takes a giant bite out of your revenue.

Customers often hire price gougers during times of crisis. They may have received a bad online rating or review. They're looking for the fastest resolution possible and believe reputation management companies are best equipped to take care of their current dilemma. For the most part, the practices price gougers employ won't harm your business, and unlike the extortion scheme outlined above, they weren't responsible for perpetrating it in the first place.

Nevertheless, the adage "You get what you pay for" doesn't apply when it comes to price gougers. Similar services are available from other providers for a smaller fee, so shopping around is the only way to ensure you're getting the best possible deal and advice.

Disappearing Acts: Here Today...

In addition to the high cost of reputation management services, another common problem can surface.

Imagine you've just found out a customer posted a scathing online review. Panicked, you search the Internet for guidance. You learn about reputation management companies and how they can help you. Without knowing how to separate solid companies from lousy ones, you hastily hire one based on the testimonials on its site and on the promise (even sometimes accompanied with a money-back guarantee) that the company will get the job done for you.

The problem with some of the companies that advertise these services is that they may employ black hat SEO trickery in an attempt to fool search engines, rating-and-review sites, and other online platforms into ignoring harmful content and promoting helpful content.

> If you hire one of these companies, you're inviting the wrath of a thousand black-magic cyber witches whose electronic trickery can forever damage your business.

These consultants and companies may charge you thousands of dollars for their services. In exchange you may receive a Yelp profile stuffed with fake reviews, which, if you're caught, can earn you a Yelp public shaming (such as that suffered by Dan W., as described on page 36)—a reminder to you and the web-surfing public of the horrible decision you made.

If Google catches on to what you're up to, the world's largest search engine may penalize you by dropping your ranking in search engine results. The result is *fewer* web visitors to your own site and *more* web visitors to your Yelp and other rating-and-review site profiles—ones that may be marked with dreaded electronic scarlet letters. And the news gets worse.

Disappearing Acts: Gone Tomorrow

By the time you find out about the damage inflicted by the reputation management company you hired, that company will be long gone. The email address you used to correspond with the company is no longer active. The phone number, if the company ever had one at all, is disconnected. It seems the consultant or company disappeared without any trace.

Now that you've paid thousands of dollars to a company that has tarnished your online reputation, you're left without anyone to blame and no one to honor your money-back guarantee.

On the *pure evil* spectrum, companies such as these aren't as diabolical as the scam artists who threaten to post damaging fake reviews on your site and then implore you to hire them for reputation management.

But the point is, you should always practice caution when it comes to hiring a reputation management company or consultant. If you believe you are in need of these services, you may wish to jump ahead to Chapter 11 to learn more about what questions you should ask and how to choose one that fits your particular needs.

Better yet, take control and implement the strategies outlined in this book today, before you face a crisis needing urgent attention. This way, you'll never be pressured into seeking these services out of desperation and vulnerability.

They're Here to Stay—Make Them Work for You

You're at the center of one of the world's most profitable web-based platforms. Without businesses such as yours, the rating-and-review industry would disappear in an instant. But barring the entire Internet's collapse, you cannot turn away from the rating-and-review industry.

In fact, as the Internet expands, so will the rating-and-review sites that support it. In the next chapter, you'll learn about businesses just like yours that are embracing rating-and-review sites and leveraging them to their benefit.

5

The Choice Is Yours

· ·

In the blockbuster film *The Matrix*, Laurence Fishburne's Morpheus gives Keanu Reeves's Neo two choices, the outcome of which will forever influence Neo's life. Swallow a blue pill and accept the status quo, or take a red pill to unveil new opportunities.

You face a similar decision when it comes to rating-and-review sites. On the one hand, you have the choice to take the blue pill.

In this chapter, you'll learn:

✔ How businesses are using rating-and-review sites to dramatically boost revenue

✔ The true rewards of mastering your online rating-and-review strategy

You might say, "Rating-and-review sites are hurdles to my success, but managing them is time consuming and overwhelming."

I don't fault business owners who choose the comfort of inaction over the uncertainty of embarking on a new marketing path. As a small business owner myself, I understand the temptation to dive into the other 2,001 items on my business owner to-do list rather than focus my efforts on something that may become time consuming with no guarantee of success.

With that said, the fact you're reading this book means you're dissatisfied with the status quo and open to finding new solutions. So let's take your curiosity a step further and imagine you've hired me to help you make the most of your marketing efforts.

During our initial meeting, I'd listen to your concerns, fears, and complaints, many of which I identified in previous chapters. I'd also empathize with your reluctance and trepidation related to taking action. Next, I'd dish out some tough love:

> *Your choice was made when you decided to open a business.*
> *In other words, you don't have a damn choice in the matter.*

By neglecting to take control of your online ratings and reviews, you're creating barriers for customers to find you and learn about you. Competition in your industry is fierce, so why make it even harder for your prospects to understand what you have to offer?

> *Ignoring rating-and-review sites is as harmful to your*
> *business as shutting off your phone service or taking down*
> *your store sign.*

As unbelievable as this may sound to many of you, your top source of new customers *is* rating-and-review sites. So sitting idly by will harm you by reducing your business's long-term prospects.

Now that you know the consequences of not participating in the rating-and-review game, let's explore the benefits of challenging it. No doubt, online rating-and-review platforms favor reviewers over your business's interests. And they often turn a blind eye to reviewers who misbehave and post inaccurate information about your business.

Despite these significant and frustrating obstacles, actively participating in your online reputation provides a massive opportunity for your business, as you'll soon see.

A Case Study in Leveraging Rating-and-Review Sites

In 2008, when Andrew DiFeo launched his Hyundai dealership in St. Augustine, Florida, he was bullish about growth. Within a little over two decades, the South Korean–based automobile manufacturer had gone from an unknown in the automotive industry to a powerful brand known for high-quality cars with cutting-edge design.

If you remember what it was like in 2008—banking crisis, housing crisis, stock market crisis—you'll quickly realize that DiFeo's Hyundai dealership launched at a time of unprecedented economic headwind. While he was certainly moving merchandise, he wasn't pleased with selling just fifty cars per month. The intrepid entrepreneur knew his business could do better.

DiFeo understood that for auto dealers, over 70 percent of a consumer's dealer decision was based on online ratings and reviews, and many of them came from DealerRater. As a result, he focused his marketing budget, time, and effort on rating-and-review sites.

He took an objective and honest look at what his customers were saying about his business on DealerRater. He learned to embrace all ratings and reviews—positive and negative—and address problem areas immediately. He even discovered that unfavorable reviews were actually good for business.

"We need bad reviews," said DiFeo. "It's an odd thing, but it adds credibility."

By addressing customer service issues and responding to negative reviews, he turned around his company's fortunes. In fact, DealerRater named his business Dealer of the Year for three years in a row (2010, 2011, and 2012). He also captured positive, balanced reviews on other sites relevant to his business, such as Edmunds, Cars.com, and Google.

Most importantly, his dealership more than doubled its sales volume. But rather than sit on his success, he continued to use feedback from online rating-and-review sites to improve customer service.

DiFeo's even-keeled attitude about online ratings and reviews reflects the reality that no matter how hard you work, your rating-

and-review problems will not go away. And it is guaranteed that not every reviewer will give high marks.

"Does it sting when you get a negative review? Of course, especially for the first few. Then you realize that this is reality and that you're not going to satisfy 100 percent of people 100 percent of the time," he noted.

Keeping Your Eye on the Prize

This book will show you how to effectively manage the online ratings and reviews of your business. But let me be precise about the ultimate goal here.

The goal is *not* for you to be great at managing ratings and reviews.

This is probably a relief for those of you who'd rather spend time and energy on the core elements of your business.

The true goal is for you to be great at your business because you've mastered and reaped the benefits of what ratings and reviews can do to improve your business.

Of the many benefits to be enjoyed, key above all is that this makes you great at listening to customers. Online ratings and reviews are a gold mine of free feedback and advice from the experts who really matter—your customers.

Don't fear this platform. Embrace it! Actively shift your attention away from the distractions and challenges this industry presents and focus instead on the voices of your customers. Through their reviews, they're trying to tell you what's working and what needs attention with your business. If you can do this, you'll outmaneuver even the most intimidating aspects of this industry and, ultimately, be better at your business because of it.

Time to Start Your Challenge

Now that you understand how and why the rating-and-review sites have left your business manipurated, you're armed with the background necessary to change your course and steer your business in the right direction.

Part Two of *Manipurated* will give you the nuts and bolts of how you'll succeed.

Part Two: Tools and Tactics

If you've read *Manipurated* this far you should now have a grasp of the broader landscape of the rating-and-review industry.

On one hand, you can view rating-and-review websites as a necessary evil—another hoop to jump through when doing business. On the other hand, you've seen examples of how these sites can actually boosted business owners' bottom lines and profits.

Rather than resist the inevitable electronic tide, Part Two of this book shows you how to leverage your online ratings and reviews for success. In the chapters that follow, you'll learn powerful principles that have increased revenues and decreased stress for business owners across the country—men and women just like you.

What's In It for You?

You've hopefully internalized by now the tremendous opportunities that online rating-and-review sites offer to your business. Still need another nudge? Then indulge me in the following math that will make very clear that we're talking real dollars and cents:

Let's say your business has an annual gross profit of $500,000.

Now, for the sake of this scenario, imagine you pledged to commit one year to focus on your online ratings and reviews following the principles you'll learn about in Part Two of *Manipurated*.

What will your payout be?

If you're in the restaurant business, you've read that a single star increase in your overall rating can result in a 5 to 9 percent boost in revenue. In our $500,000 scenario, that means you'll earn from $25,000 to $45,000 *more* every year.

That's real money, and it's worth being excited about. Think what you could do with that extra income: upgrade equipment, remodel your retail space or office, increase support staff, or take an incredible vacation. It's your money that is being left on the table.

So are you ready to reap these rewards? If your answer is "Yes," Part Two will fill your personal rating-and-review site toolbox with resources and skills that are designed around your busy life. It won't require a degree in computer science. In fact, making the rating-and-review sites work for you is easier than you think.

How to Navigate Part Two of This Book

To save you time, I've organized the chapters in Part Two in a way that will allow you to customize your strategy. Think of it as your own personal rating-and-review coach at your service! Feel free to read all of Part Two from beginning to end. Or, if you're strapped for time and looking for quick solutions, pick and choose the chapters relevant to your present needs.

Shortcuts

☞ Want a deeper understanding of the rating-and-review world's jargon? Curious what the most common reviewer personality types are? Then start with Chapter 6 (page 54).

☞ Have an uncertain or shaky grasp about what's being said about your business today? Start with Chapter 7 (page 70).

☞ Bogged down with a bunch of bad reviews? Ready for solutions to fight back? Start with Chapter 8 (page 86).

☞ Seeking to increase positive reviews, but can't figure out how? Read Chapter 9 (page 99).

☞ The beneficiary of glorious reviews? Good for you. Go show them off and grow your business! Start with Chapter 10 (page 116).

☞ Convinced or suspicious something's just not right with some existing reviews about your business? Start with Chapter 11 (page 126).

6

Business Owner's Toolbox: How to Win

. . . .

Everything of significance you've ever built in your life—relationships, business, family—has required starting with a solid foundation. Developing a successful online rating-and-review strategy is no different.

This chapter outlines the basic tools that you'll use over and over during your journey. These tools will help you understand the bigger context for all of the steps you're about to read. The four essential items in the toolbox are:

In this chapter, you'll learn:

✔ How the *Manipurated* Code of Conduct will help you prosper

✔ About the most important rating-and-review sites

✔ What the main rating-and-review personality types are

- The *Manipurated* Code of Conduct
- Familiarity with the top rating-and-review sites
- Fluency in the common terminology used in this book and the online rating-and-review industry
- Understanding the personality types who are reviewing you

The *Manipurated* Code of Conduct

The first of these tools I call the *Manipurated* Code of Conduct. Similar to a construction site's requirement that all participants abide by a set of fundamental rules in order to engender safety, avoid accidents, and keep the project moving ahead smoothly without delay, the role of the *Manipurated* Code of Conduct is to increase your likelihood of experiencing amazing outcomes. In order to make this process work for you, you must commit to these tenets:

I pledge to:

☞ **Practice good review hygiene every day.** Like brushing my teeth, this is a non-negotiable daily practice. I understand that good review hygiene prevents unsightly bad review buildup and brings about better results overall.

☞ **Take this commitment seriously.** Although no one ever asked my permission to post ratings and reviews about my business, I acknowledge they are important to my customers, which means they're also important to me.

☞ **Avoid taking reviews personally.** Separating business life from personal life will help me do this. I admit it's hard not to be offended, hurt, sad, or downright angry when someone posts a negative review—especially because I've poured my heart and soul into my business at great personal and financial risk. Despite this, I will remember that business is business.

☞ **Follow necessary steps and not cut corners.** I've invested my life and livelihood into my business, so as far as managing my online ratings and reviews is concerned, there are no shortcuts. This is a long-term business strategy. As with anything worth having in life, this requires consistent focus.

The Site Landscape

The second item in the toolbox is understanding the characteristics of the top rating-and-review sites. I've summarized the key features of the top fifteen sites below, along with their written review requirements. Keep this page as a reference for your exploration of the chapters in this part of the book.

General Local Businesses

Company Name: Angie's List
Web Address: www.angieslist.com
Types of Content: Requires written comments and a variety of detailed comments.
Area of Focus: Services
Founded: 1996
Annual Revenue: $315 million

Angie's List is a subscription-only service to help consumers find detailed reviews on roofers, plumbers, dentists, and other service providers. Its more than 3 million members check the website before they hire a service provider. The reviews come from real people who are paid members of the site, not anonymous users. Angie's List has ratings and reviews in more than 720 home repair and health care services. Reviews on the site capture a variety of data, including when the work was completed and the approximate cost.

Company Name: Citysearch
Web Address: www.citysearch.com
Types of Content: Thumbs up/thumbs down ratings and reviews permitted independent of each other.
Area of Focus: Dining, entertainment, professional services
Founded: 1995
Annual Revenue: Unknown

Citysearch is an online guide that provides information about businesses in the categories of dining, entertainment, retail, travel, and professional services in cities throughout the United States. Visitors to each of Citysearch's local city guides will find contact information, maps, driving directions, and editorial and user reviews for the businesses listed. Citysearch is unique in the way it ranks businesses because its rankings are based on both consumer reviews and editorial reviews by its staff.

General Local Businesses *continued*

· ·

Company Name: Facebook
Web Address: www.facebook.com
Types of Content: Star ratings only, no embedded reviews.
Area of Focus: All business types
Founded: 2004
Annual Revenue: $12.5 billion

Facebook's business pages have built-in ratings (enabled in the Local Businesses category).

· ·

Company Name: Foursquare
Web Address: www.foursquare.com
Types of Content: Captures ratings in binary fashion (like/don't like). Comments separate.
Area of Focus: Restaurants, entertainment
Founded: 2009
Annual Revenue: $20 million (2013)

Foursquare is designed as a highly personalized local recommendation service. Combined with Swarm, its other product, it enables consumers to discover places that may be of interest to them in their local community and to plan meet-ups with friends. Ratings are part of the Foursquare product.

· ·

Company Name: Google My Business
Web Address: www.google.com/business
Types of Content: Allows star ratings without comments.
Area of Focus: All business types
Founded: 2014
Annual Revenue: Unknown

Google My Business is a fast and easy way for businesses, products, brands, artists, and organizations to manage their online presence with Google. Previously known as Google Local.

· ·

Company Name: Yahoo Local
Web Address: local.yahoo.com
Types of Content: Reviews provided by Yelp.
Area of Focus: All business types
Founded: 2013
Annual Revenue: Unknown

Yahoo Local is an online local advertising system that gives businesses the ability to provide detailed business information to millions of potential customers. Basic listings are free of charge. It offers premium services for businesses that prefer additional listing features.

· ·

General Local Businesses *continued*

. . . .

Company Name: Yelp
Web Address: www.yelp.com
Types of Content: Requires written comments.
Area of Focus: Local businesses
Founded: 2004
Annual Revenue: $377 million

Yelp connects people primarily with local businesses. Yelp had a monthly average of 135 million unique visitors[1] in the fourth quarter of 2014, 72 million of whom accessed the website via their mobile devices. By the end of 2014, Yelp had more than 71 million local reviews, making Yelp the leading local guide for real word of mouth on everything from boutiques and mechanics to restaurants and dentists.

. . . .

Company Name: Zomato (previously UrbanSpoon)
Web Address: www.zomato.com
Types of Content: Captures ratings in binary fashion (like/don't like). Reviews curated from Zomato users and the web.
Area of Focus: Restaurants
Founded: 2006 (UrbanSpoon founding)
Annual Revenue: Unknown

Zomato is a global restaurant search and discovery service. It officially launched in North America in 2015 when it acquired UrbanSpoon. Available on the web and through mobile apps.

. . . .

Automotive

. . . .

Company Name: DealerRater
Web Address: www.dealerrater.com
Types of Content: Written comments required. Accepts reviews from anonymous sources.
Area of Focus: Car dealerships
Founded: 2002
Annual Revenue: Over $14 million (2013)

DealerRater is the world's no. 1 online resource for anyone seeking trusted third-party information on automobile dealerships. DealerRater features 41,000 U.S. and Canadian car dealers, nearly 2 million consumer reviews, and over 1 million cars for sale. DealerRater attracts more than 12 million consumers every year who visit the site to search for car dealerships, read reviews, write their own descriptive reviews, and find car deals.

. . . .

---

1 Unique visitors: Distinct individuals who visited a website during a given time period, regardless of how often they visited.

Health Care

Company Name: Healthgrades
Web Address: www.healthgrades.com
Types of Content: Completed survey required (with email/text confirmation). Anonymous submission accepted.
Area of Focus: Physicians, hospitals, and health care providers
Founded: 1998
Annual Revenue: Unknown

Healthgrades's mission is to help consumers find the right doctor and the right hospital, for the right care. More than 1 million people a day rely on Healthgrades to research, compare, and connect with physicians and other health care professionals.

Company Name: Vitals
Web Address: www.vitals.com
Types of Content: Comments not required. Accepts reviews from anonymous sources.
Area of Focus: Health care
Founded: 2007
Annual Revenue: $14 million (2013)

Vitals provides ratings and reviews of physicians and other medical providers in a wide variety of categories. It has built-in review monitoring services for health care providers to keep track of their reputation.

Company Name: ZocDoc
Web Address: www.zocdoc.com
Types of Content: Written comments required and only from verified patients.
Area of Focus: Health care
Founded: 2007
Annual Revenue: Unknown

ZocDoc is a combined online booking service and reviews platform. It permits physicians to take bookings for appointments online and provides patients with reviews of physicians from other ZocDoc users.

Legal

. . . .

Company Name: Avvo
Web Address: www.avvo.com
Types of Content: Written comments required.
Area of Focus: Lawyers
Founded: 2007
Annual Revenue: $1 to $2.5 million

Avvo is the leading legal online marketplace, making legal dealings easier by connecting consumers and lawyers. Avvo's lawyer directory provides Avvo-rated profiles, client reviews, and peer endorsements for 97 percent of all lawyers in the United States, so consumers can find the lawyer who's right for them. Avvo also helps lawyers grow their businesses with marketing tools and services, including the Avvo JD App and Avvo Ignite, a cloud-based marketing platform designed specifically for attorneys.

Travel and Tourism

. . . .

Company Name: Amazon
Web Address: www.amazon.com
Types of Content: Requires written comments (hotels only as of mid-2015).
Area of Focus: E-commerce and travel (2015)
Founded: 1994
Annual Revenue: $89 billion

Amazon is a vast marketplace for products. Generally an e-commerce platform, Amazon recently launched a travel product (Amazon Destinations) to allow consumers to book local trip experiences.

Company Name: TripAdvisor
Web Address: www.tripadvisor.com
Types of Content: Written comments required.
Area of Focus: Travel and tourism, restaurants
Founded: 2000
Annual Revenue: $1.2 billion

TripAdvisor claims it is the world's largest travel site. TripAdvisor captures more than 315 million unique monthly visitors, and more than 200 million reviews and opinions covering more than 4.5 million accommodations, restaurants, and attractions.

A Breakdown of Ratings and Reviews

There are a few key differences between ratings and reviews.

Ratings are quick, nonnarrative representations of a consumer's experience with your business, usually using a concise visual aid or grade. Ratings are most commonly depicted as stars, numeric scores, or letter grades.

Compared with reviews, ratings are generally more passive. They may lack context if there is no written comment (in other words, a review) attached to them, so you don't know precisely what caused the customer to give you a certain star count or score.

Ratings are very important in search results on Google and elsewhere, as they are presented alongside your business information. When a consumer searches for your business and sees the search result, he or she may also see a rating next to or under your name. Because of their high visibility, you need to be just as focused on your ratings as you are on your written reviews.

Reviews, on the other hand, are the written comments. They allow consumers to use their own words to describe their interaction and express their opinions in greater detail. They are generally only a few paragraphs in length.

Because they describe a customer's experience with your business, this is where insights about your business originate, and they are where you probably experience the biggest battles for control of your message.

Some online platforms require consumers to give both a rating and a written review. Meanwhile, others require only a rating and written comments are optional. When possible, encourage your customers to give both a rating and a review.

Manipurated Key Terms

The third tool in your toolbox is gaining a command of the key terminology used in this book and by the industry at large.

Authenticate: The act of signing in, logging in, or confirming credentials to a website to verify identity.

Black Hat SEO: Deceitful tactics used by the SEO industry designed to induce higher rankings on search engines. Might include creating fake webs of links or stuffing keywords on a page in an attempt to trick algorithms into believing a site is trustworthy.

Bot (or zombie) attacks: Bot is short for robot. These are automated, repetitious reviews or actions taken on a site by bots disguised (often poorly) as humans. Examples include reviews submitted to an online rating-and-review site stuffed with links or keywords. Because bots, zombies, and other nonhumans post content, they're often poorly written.

Claim: The act of taking ownership of a profile on a rating-and-review site. Generally speaking, this is an indication to the site operator that you are the owner of the business being profiled. Claiming a listing typically allows you access to additional features and controls on the rating-and-review site.

Flagging: An action taken on a rating-and-review site to tag a specific review as fraudulent, fake, or otherwise in violation of the site's terms and conditions. Most sites denote a flagging capability with a small flag icon. Some sites have a fine-print link that says "flag this post" or something similar.

Flame: A malicious written attack on a business or individual on the Internet. Flames originated in online chat rooms and forums. Often used in verb form, as in to "flame" someone.

Flamebait: A negative, hateful post or comment designed to elicit anger and start an online argument. Flamebait often includes incendiary language and hyperbole to pick a fight.

Funny, Useful, and Cool (FUC): You'll find three buttons—funny, useful, and cool—at the bottom of each Yelp review. Active Yelpers thrive on their reviews being FUC'd. Often, reviews are written to elicit one of these three votes, and high-ranking Yelp reviewers will have high percentages of FUC'd reviews.

Search Engine Marketing (SEM): Fee-based, paid search listings that appear at the top or side of most search engine listings. Businesses must pay to be included. SEM is focused on the part of the search results that are referred to as paid search.

Search Engine Optimization (SEO): Focused on the part of the search results known as organic search. These are the actual search results derived by the search engine's automated algorithm. This is called organic because the search results aren't influenced by paid efforts or advertising like SEM. Optimization of a business's pages to secure better and more favorable positions in organic search is further classified as black hat SEO (see "black hat") or white hat SEO (see "white hat").

SERP: Stands for "search engine results page," which refers to the organic search results for a specific search query. Used in reference to where your business ranks, as in "You are no. 1 on the SERP for the 'plumbers Austin' keyword."

Sock Puppet: Fake identities created to promote a business or person through online reviews, mentions, and posts. They are designed to mimic real people with real profiles.

Spam: Unsolicited, automated, and otherwise garbage content on the Internet. Spam is often generated by bots (see "Bot attacks").

Terms of Service (TOS): Sometimes referred to as "terms and conditions" or "terms of use." This is the lengthy online fine print that reviewers frequently neglect to read. It comprises rules that one must agree to in order to use a particular site or service.

Troll: Usually people who try to mislead or lure other Internet users into heated conversation. They operate with anonymous usernames and are almost impossible to track down. They like to start fights.

White Hat SEO: In contrast to black hat SEO, white hat SEO comprises tactics and techniques that boost ranking on a search engine via legitimate, authority-building tactics.

Yelpers: Active reviewers on the Yelp platform. They often focus on achieving higher reviewer status and FUC votes. Yelp Elite is the top echelon of this group. They represent the platform's most active Yelpers.

Who Are Your Reviewers?

The fourth and final item in your toolbox is identifying the key personality types that fit most reviewers. Understanding how a customer thinks will help frame how you deal with a particular review, including how to formulate the best response. The four personality types below are in addition to the fake reviewers I have addressed earlier in the book (see page 33).

The Regulars

These reviewers are loyal patrons of your business. They are probably some of your favorite customers, because they are repeat customers. They're also likely to refer you to others. Because they purchase from you often, they're in a good place to offer feedback, critiques, and suggestions about your business. You might think of the Regulars as your "bread-and-butter" customers.

The Desperate Outcriers

Reviews from Desperate Outcriers are bound to sting and poke at open wounds. The reviewers pointing out these weaknesses are letting you know you've done something to upset them, and their negative review is their way (albeit a passive-aggressive one) to inform you that you've gone down the wrong path.

Here's the shocking part about Desperate Outcriers: they are written by your best and most loyal customers.

Their reviews usually express frustration with an experience that they would like to have gone better. Most recount a story that's reasonable and shows an effort at remediating a problem unsuccessfully. If you read carefully what they have to say, you're likely to find a diagnostic pearl that will help your business do better next time.

What they need, more than anything, is to feel heard. Yes, you'd prefer that they called you instead of flaming you online, but they may see it differently. They may feel that they've already tried other feedback paths. By monitoring your profile regularly, you might catch their review early and intervene quickly to make things right.

What they say may feel very critical, and how they say it may feel hurtful. When your feelings are hurt, or you're frustrated or angry, remind yourself of *Manipurated* Code of Conduct item three:

I pledge to avoid taking reviews personally.

The following is a potential Desperate Outcry for a mortuary service in Inglewood, California:

Losing my brother was a hard enough thing to experience, but these people, particularly Dr. Black, was so disrespectful and unprofessional that he made me regret having ever gone to them for help with my funeral needs. Once I reported his blatant disrespect, the manager Derrick King was a little more professional and had better customer service skills. The receptionist was the most friendly and helpful person there. After leaving there, I felt like I had been kicked while I was down. I will be filing a complaint with the better business bureau.

At first glance, you may think that this is an angry customer who hates your business and whom you've lost forever. But look more closely. Though the overall tone is down, this Desperate Outcrier's review is balanced and not altogether unreasonable.

The consumer clearly attempted to address his or her disappointment with Dr. Black. Even though things didn't go as the reviewer liked, the reviewer had some praise for things that he or she appreciated; indeed, the writer even suggested that Derrick King and the receptionist were helpful.

Even though the review threatened to lodge a complaint, odds are that at the time the review was posted, this had not yet been done.

If you were the mortuary owner, you should immediately see this as an urgent situation. You should post a response apologizing for the experience, which lets other consumers see that you're on top of the issue. You should attempt to reach the consumer directly to address their concerns. And above all, you should seek to understand exactly what it was about the experience that was disappointing.

Desperate Outcriers do not post reviews solely to attack the business. Quite the contrary, they post a review as a desperate plea for help. If you promptly and skillfully answer this plea, chances are good you'll turn a Desperate Outcrier into a fan.

The Socialites

Socialites write reviews for fun and ego. They see rating-and-review sites as a virtual community where their contributions help others on the site explore the world. They frequently review different categories of products and businesses as they work to amass a large amount of reviews. They may not buy from you regularly, but they contribute to the review platform they're on regularly. These could be seen as popular Yelpers, for example. They're in it for their own self-promotion.

They see their involvement in online rating-and-review sites as a platform for personal enrichment, professional advancement, or both. As a result, they set their eyes on top-dog rating-and-review site status such as membership in the Yelp Elite program detailed in Chapter 2. Their reviews are the criteria by which the rating-and-review sites will judge them.

Yelp has fueled the aspirations and competitive nature of Socialites through online challenges. For example, in 2013, it played host to the Yelp 100 Challenge, which had the following rules:

1. *You have three choices: Click "I'm in!" "Sounds Cool," or retreat back into Internet obscurity where I will never bother you again.*

2. *If you do join the challenge, the goal is to write 100 AWESOME reviews by the end of the year. We're not in it for the mediocrity; we're in it for the glory. Any business (even a business you visit while traveling) is fair game, as long as the review has good and useful content.*

3. *Make a list on your profile titled "Yelp 100 Challenge!" add your 2013 reviews to the list, and update us all on your progress from time to time!*

4. *Continue being awesome.*

The Yelp reviewer below has participated in the Yelp 100 program and sees herself as the oracle of boba tea advice for Northern California. Note that this is an actual review for a real boba tea stand. As this typical Socialite review demonstrates, reading it gives you a better sense of the reviewer's personality than the business itself:

BOBA PRINCESS APPROVED with preliminary caution and advice! :P

TL;DR?? Although the billionth boba shop in the Alvarado Niles plaza, Sharetea still reigns supreme in quality. Shaky and spotty in service but they have great customer service. If you're fine with the kinks, then visit UC Sharetea now! Currently in its Soft Opening stages, they will Officially Open in about a week with BOGO deals! Yayuh! GET THE CREAMAS.

> The ever expanding Sharetea has graced us South
> Bay with a location in Union City! I hope they're
> in the works of opening one in SAN JOSE *cough
> hint hint*
>
> Good Milk Tea & Boba Quality (Grade A): CHECK
> Reasonable Prices (~$4 per drink w/topping): CHECK
> FAST & FRIENDLY Service: Half-Check
> Great Location: CHECK
> Trendy Cool Ambiance: Half-Check

If you can cut through the Boba Princess Approved verbiage (itself sort of a foreign language), there might be some real feedback for the business owner. Taken as a whole, though, it's primarily focused on improving the author's standing in the Yelp community. The review is as much about her as it is about the business.

The Snipers

Sadly, these reviewers never heard their parents say, "If you can't say anything nice, don't say anything at all." Or maybe they did, but their personality disorders kept them from heeding the parental advice.

The bottom line is you'd be hard pressed to find they like *anything*—on or offline. Snipers wear their acrid review language as a dysfunctional badge of dishonor. While they may not necessarily be out to get you, they'll certainly be willing to draw you into their dark world.

In the real world, business owners would label Snipers as "high maintenance," "troublemakers," and "ones who didn't receive enough hugs growing up" the moment they walk in the store's front door. Snipers think their negative emotional state makes them funny or stand out. They're so snarky that you don't wish them even on your worst enemy.

Almost without fail they are going to have gripes about your business. You can't win with this crowd. They may not see their immediate role as one designed to take you down (these aren't fake reviewers, just unstable ones). But if you happen to come across them, they may unleash aggressively on your business on rating-and-review sites.

You've seen them:

I waited TWENTY MINUTES for my pizza to be ready when it was supposed to be done when I got there. Then it was too hot to carry back to my car. It made my seat sweaty it was so hot! As if that wasn't enough, they put the pepperoni UNDER the cheese so it doesn't even get crispy. Fail on all counts.

Encounters with Snipers really challenge you to draw on your pledge not to take reviews personally. For this personality type in particular, take consolation knowing that *no one*, including you, is able to please them.

On pages 96–98, you will find specific examples of how to respond to Snipers and the other personality types.

Understanding the mind-set of your reviewers not only impacts how you react to reviews they've already written but also influences how you go about generating more reviews for your business. As you read through the rest of Part Two, keep these personality types in mind.

7

Where to See and Be Seen

What's Being Said About You Online and Where It Matters

As a business owner trying to manage your online ratings and reviews, one of your first questions is probably "What's being said about my business online?"

To answer this question, you first have to know where to look, meaning *where* are things being said about your business. But as you know, the Internet is a big place. For most small business owners, scouring the vast pages of the web for mentions of your business isn't a practical strategy. And if you end up finding that your business is mentioned on many different sites, how can you determine which ones matter the most?

In this chapter, you'll learn:

✔ How to find ratings and reviews of your business online

✔ Which online sites actually drive customer visits to your website

✔ Where you should focus your rating-and-review efforts

✔ How to claim and update information about your business on the top rating-and-review sites

Here's some good news—you don't have to monitor every site you find. Keep in mind that just because a site contains information about your business doesn't mean that people are actually finding that site, let alone being influenced by it.

Instead of venturing off to discover every corner of the web where your business is mentioned, ask yourself a more important question: "Which websites actually drive real business my way?" If you can answer this question, you'll be able to focus your resources on the places that lead customers to your website and, ultimately, your front door. These are the places your business needs to see and be seen.

Goal One: Determine Where Your Customers Find You

This issue of identifying what sites influence your customers is essential to your sanity and your time management. Without this knowledge, you'll be tempted to surf from site to site, attempting to get involved and engaged at every mention of your company.

The good news is that learning where your customers find you is remarkably easy.

If you are an active online marketer, you may have already done this research and know what sites influence your customers. If that is the case, you can just skim the steps ahead—but please take the time to fill in the My Top Priority Rating-and-Review Sites chart on page 76, as you'll refer back to it in later chapters.

If you don't know how your customers are finding you, then grab your computer and get started addressing this goal, following these four steps. The objective of each can be summarized as follows:

1. Perform an incognito search to get a snapshot of all the online sites where your business is mentioned on the Internet, especially those with ratings and reviews.
2. Determine which of these sites are actually driving customers to your website.
3. Confirm with actual customers which rating-and-review site they used to find you.

4. Analyze the overlap of steps 1, 2, and 3 to determine which rating-and-review sites are top priorities for your business.

(The software required for these operations is all free. It just requires a little investment of your time.)

Step 1: The Incognito Search

For this step, I'm sending you on a secret mission. If you accept this undercover operation, you'll be required to conduct a secret search.

On your web browser, you'll need to use what I'll broadly describe as *private mode*. Under this setting, you eliminate any personalization of the search results that could change or personalize the search results that you will see. This keeps the search as neutral as possible, minimizing the chances that your results differ from what other people would see.

While the concept of private mode is the same for all browsers, it's called by different names. It may be referred to as *incognito mode* or *private window* or something similar. If you have trouble figuring out what your browser calls it, refer to this helpful About.com article that should point you in the right direction:

> Resource: browsers.about.com/od/faq/tp/Incognito-Browsing.htm

Once you've activated the incognito mode for your browser, go to Google and do a search for your business. Because you are browsing privately, Google will not personalize any of the results it shows you. If you repeat the search on your normal browser window, and are logged in to a Google account when you do it, you might notice that different search results show up displaying different content.

When the incognito mode search results come up, what are the top two to four results? You might find a link to your website, a link or two to rating-and-review sites, or even a link to an article or blog post about your business.

Because other Internet users are seeing these same results when they search for your business, these top several sites will frame the majority of your web-browsing audiences' opinions about your business.

The Bigger Picture

An Internet search for your business may reveal mentions on a cornucopia of sources beyond rating-and-review sites. Keep in mind that ratings and reviews are part of a bigger online landscape that includes blogs, social media sites like Facebook and Twitter, news sites, and possibly other forums where your business might be mentioned. Though *Manipurated* guides you on the ins and outs of rating-and-review sites, you may wish to include these other sites in your analysis.

Research shows that consumers are most likely to click the top two to four search results.

If you have a restaurant or retail business, most likely Yelp appears at the top of your search results. You may also find Citysearch, Zomato, MenuPages, or even editorial reviews from your local newspaper within the top four.

Take your top rating-and-review search results from this step and list them in the circle labeled "Search Findings" in the chart provided on page 76.

Step 2: Google Analytics

Now you need to determine which sites actually lead customers to click through to your own website. The only two prerequisites for this next step are that you:

1. Have a business website that you maintain
2. Have installed or started using Google Analytics to track the site traffic

For most businesses, Google Analytics is the best available tool to track website traffic and analyze trends related to a website. It requires a very simple installation process, so if someone else is managing your website, you may need to inquire about whether Google Analytics is being used (and if not, what it takes to get it installed).

Once logged in to Google Analytics you want to find within Google Analytics' labyrinth of reports one titled "Source/Medium" (see Figure 7.1). To make it easy to find, Google Analytics has a search bar in the upper left corner. To find this report, enter the search term "Source/Medium" and Google Analytics will give you a direct link to the report.

Now that you're on the report page, you have the choice to view different reporting periods. You'll find an option to set a particular date range in the upper right corner of the site's page. For the purposes of your rating-and-review strategy, go back to it every three to six months, which should give you a comprehensive snapshot of your average website visitor free from possible short-term variances due to seasonality, promotions, or other outside influences.

Figure 7.1. Google Source/Medium Report

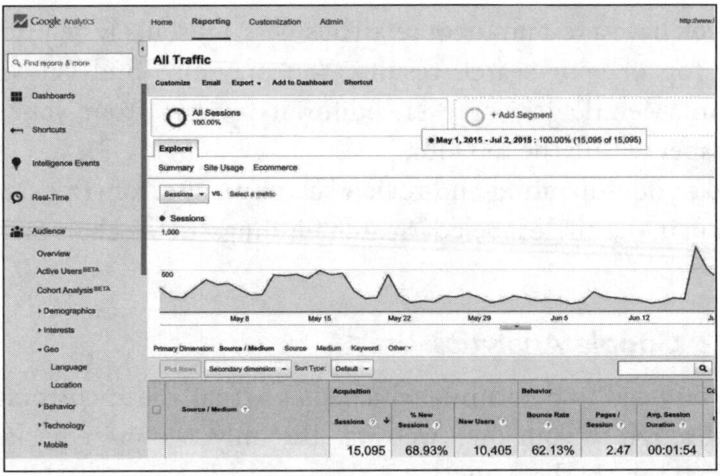

The Source/Medium report describes where the visitors to your website are coming from. In most cases, you'll see the top source of your website traffic listed as "direct/none" and "google/organic." You may also see social networks such as Facebook and Twitter listed here.

Your purpose for looking through this report is focused, for now, on identifying rating-and-review sites that drive traffic to your website. To find them, continue to scroll down the list and look for any online rating-and-review sites. Keep an eye out for sites such as Yelp, TripAdvisor, and Citysearch in your list of traffic sources. See one or more of these sites?

What their presence tells you is that the rating-and-review site is driving customers to your website's front door—the number in the chart will give you an indication of how many. It may not be a large number, but its presence in the report is important as it indicates the site in question is a traffic generator for you.

Take the top two to four rating-and-review sites from this step and list them in the circle labeled "Google Analytics Findings" in the chart on page 76.

Step 3: Customer Confirmation

The information from steps 1 and 2 is helpful, but to get final confirmation, you go to the source—your customers.

It's now time to shake hands and strike up a conversation with your prospects and customers. This decidedly offline step involves asking one refreshingly straightforward question:

Where did you find me?

Ask it when you meet your customers, either over the phone, by email, or face-to-face, somewhere in the course of your interaction.

Rather than compiling enough data to make it worthy of submitting to *Nature,* just spend a couple of weeks informally asking customers how they found you. Their answers will verify that the insights you've gained through your online research are valid and actually reflective of your customers. Furthermore, consider this step as a way to test the information you've compiled so far. If the replies you receive correlate, you know which sites require your attention.

Take the top two to four rating-and-review sites that customers say led them to your business and list them in the circle labeled "Customer Analysis" in the chart provided on page 76.

Step 4: Determine the Overlap

In steps 1, 2, and 3, respectively, you've identified the most relevant rating-and-review sites for your business in terms of what customers find on search results, which sites steer them to your virtual doorstep, and what customers themselves say led them to your business.

Now you can determine which, of the sites you've discovered, are the most important ones that lead to real business. To do this, simply go to the chart and see where sites overlap with one another.

Take the top sites that overlap and list them in the spaces under the chart labeled My Top Priority Rating-and-Review Sites.

These should be your highest-priority sites—those that deserve the bulk of your online rating-and-review monitoring efforts. In other words, your "See and Be Seen" list.

This list represents the key sites where you should focus your rating-and-review efforts and energy.

My Top Priority Rating-and-Review Sites

DETERMINE YOUR TOP PRIORITY SITES

SEARCH FINDINGS

GOOGLE
ANALYTICS
FINDINGS

CUSTOMER
ANALYSIS

MY TOP
PRIORITY
RATING &
REVIEW SITES

Google Reviews: What You Should Know

One of the items you probably noticed in the incognito Google search results for your business is a star rating that appears under your business name.

These are based on ratings and reviews hosted on Google's own system and they *absolutely* matter to your business. Google calls its platform Google My Business. Previously, it was referred to as Google Local and Google+.

Until early 2015, Google based these star ratings on both the reviews on its own system and what it referred to as "reviews from around the web," which included Yelp, Citysearch, and others.

Google is no longer including these "reviews from around the web" in its star-rating determination. Of course, links to these other rating-and-review services will still appear in search results.

This is an important distinction for you to understand because it creates yet another (and decidedly frustrating) battleground for online ratings and reviews. Thus Google ratings and reviews are as important as those on Yelp, TripAdvisor, and elsewhere. You should consider adding Google Reviews to the chart on page 76 for this reason.

Goal Two: Learn What's Being Said About You

Now that you know what your top priorities are online, you need to determine what's being said about you now, and establish your process for monitoring these sites in the future.

You have two options to achieving that outcome. The first is what I call the "Do It Yourself" model, which is for business owners who have some computer savvy and a little extra time on their hands, but not a lot of money to spend on monthly services.

The second option is what I call the "Outsource" model, which is for business owners who have very little time and a little extra money to spend but who don't want to waste effort visiting every rating-and-review site on the Internet. These types of services are fee-based, so the trade-off is convenience for cash. In the marketing industry we refer to such services as *listening tools*.

Regardless of which path you choose, the goal is for you to have a concrete snapshot of the current mentions and discussions about your business on the sites that matter to your business the most. This will help you focus your limited time on the sites that actually send you business, allowing for maximum impact.

Option 1: DIY

The DIY (do it yourself) option is pretty straightforward. What you will need to do is visit the rating-and-review sites on your top priority list. If you haven't already taken the step of claiming the business as your own, you'll want to do that first, as it will give you expanded access to a few helpful analytics features not available to the general public. I outline the process for doing that on the Claim Your Space chart on page 84.

What you are looking for on your first visit to these sites is a snapshot of the current sentiment about your business:

- What is your star rating?
- What are customers saying about your business, your products, and your services?
- Are there any trends worth exploring, something that keeps coming up in reviews?
- Who is reviewing you, do you recognize those customer interactions, and do they seem legitimate?

Each of the rating-and-review services will provide you a limited amount of analytics, which might include historical star-rating charts, the ability to do a management response to specific reviews, your overall ranking on the site, and top comments from your reviews.

They will also alert you to new reviews posted since your last log-in. You will want to visit these sites daily to check for new reviews and to write responses. Go to Chapter 8 to get started on making the most of your new reviews.

Option 2: Outsource

This option takes advantage of professional services that give you a single dashboard summary of ratings and reviews from all sites, and also provide expanded analytics that will help you better identify trends and insights. It is a one-stop shop.

Depending on which provider you choose, some will scour only rating-and-review sites while others will scour the entire web for all types of sites that mention your business. This Outsource option is for you if you have the budget for these services but lack the time, know-how, or interest in doing this yourself.

Select a Monitoring Service

These services serve as your listening tools for mentions of your business on the Internet. There are many to choose from. To make the decision easier for you, I've broken them down to two groups— providers that specialize in monitoring only ratings and reviews, and providers that survey the broader Internet for all mentions of your business.

Rating-and-Review Tracking Specialists

These services will offer you a dashboard-style snapshot of all your ratings and reviews in one place. They are fee-based services.

Popular Rating-and-Review Tracking Services

Company Name: Reputation Ranger
Cost: Starts at $99 per month
Web Address: www.reputationranger.com

Reputation Ranger specializes in restaurants, lodging, general contractors, and automotive.

Company Name: ReviewInc
Cost: Starts at $39 per month
Web Address: www.reviewinc.com

At its lowest subscription level, ReviewInc tracks up to ten rating-and-review sites. Additional sites and features available at premium levels.

Company Name: ReviewPush
Cost: Charged per business location, starting at $29 per month
Web Address: www.reviewpush.com

ReviewPush tracks most major online rating-and-review sites with alerts when new reviews are published.

Company Name: ReviewTrackers
Cost: $49 per month; free trial available
Web Address: www.reviewtrackers.com

ReviewTrackers tracks reviews for your business across all major online rating-and-review sites. The service also alerts you by email when a new review is posted. This is available on computer, mobile, and tablet.

Company Name: Sendible
Cost: $59 per month
Web Address: www.sendible.com

Sendible tracks both social media sites and rating-and-review sites. For businesses that have a strong social media presence on Facebook or Twitter, this is a good combination option.

Company Name: Yext
Cost: $42 per month
Web Address: www.yext.com

Yext is a local business listings company. It is primarily focused on correcting and submitting business information. It also provides online review monitoring at its premium service level.

Broader Internet Surveillance Specialists

There is a whole Internet full of stuff beyond rating-and-review sites. You may have discovered this during your incognito search of your business. In addition to rating-and-review sites, your investigation likely found many other types of sites where your business turns up.

For example, you may also be actively mentioned or participating on social media sites like Facebook, Twitter, Instagram, and others where compliments and complaints may be posted.

In cases like these, it's wise to also look at comments of your business that exist on these types of sites even though they fall outside the rating-and-review platform.

Perhaps you'll find a glowing review in a local food blog if you're a restaurant owner, or a great write-up about your services on a wedding blog. This can help you put some context to the reviews you found in the previous step. This information will help you gain a broad perspective of your online reputation, beyond just the specific coverage of your business on rating-and-review sites.

A large number of tools accomplish this task, from the very basic to the very advanced. These generally look at mentions of your business on sites like news outlets, social media (Instagram, Twitter, YouTube, and elsewhere), and blogs. Essentially, these sites show you any Internet mention of you or your business.

Some of these tools are free, but most have low monthly subscription fees. To ease your search, I've provided the following recommendations:

Broader Internet Surveillance Providers

. . . .

Company Name: Mention
Cost: $29 per month, up to three keywords
Web Address: www.mention.com

This service contains mentions of you, your business, and your competitors. You define the search terms, and it displays them in near real time.

. . . .

Company Name: Rankur
Cost: Free, up to 50,000 mentions per month
Web Address: www.rankur.com

This reputation management search covers social media and all Internet-based media. A local business-specific dashboard is also available.

. . . .

Company Name: Social Mention
Cost: Free
Web Address: www.socialmention.com

This social media search engine displays results in real time from major social media sites.

....

Company Name: Topsy
Cost: Free
Web Address: www.topsy.com

If your business has a heavy Twitter presence, this is a comprehensive search tool worth exploring. It archives all Tweets back to 2006.

....

Company Name: Trackur
Cost: $97 per month
Web Address: www.trackur.com

Trackur is a keyword-driven monitoring tool that searches social media and traditional media for mentions of your business.

....

Making the Most of These Services

Once you've signed up for one of these services, what do you do with the information? The provider will begin to track mentions of your business on rating-and-review services and/or the broader Internet and inform you of them.

These sites can help you answer the following questions:

- On which sites are customers reviewing your business?
- Which rating-and-review sites seem to be generating the most comments?
- What are customers saying about your business on these sites?
- Do you see the same review posted by a customer on multiple review sites?

Goal Three: Get Your Online Information Up-to-Date

Now that you've identified the top priority rating-and-review sites and established a plan to monitor them using either the DIY or the Outsource options discussed in the previous pages, a critical next step is making sure that the information about your business on those sites is accurate. After all, these are the sites that most likely send business your way and you don't want customers calling the wrong number, sending an email to a discontinued email address, or showing up when you are not actually open.

Over the course of looking through information about your business you will probably find some information that is outdated. Perhaps Google has your store hours listed wrong or the phone number has changed. This is important information that consumers use to get in touch with you, and if it's not accurate it might cost you some lost business.

One option for doing this is to verify your information yourself one site at a time. Virtually all sites allow you to correct inaccurate details of your business. The downside to doing this yourself is that it takes a lot of time. Also, it can be tedious navigating the how-to's of updating your information on each site.

If time and effort are issues, another option is to pay someone else to do the updating for you. Not surprisingly, there's an app for this. You'll find companies dedicated to uncovering errors and omissions about your business—such as inaccurate hours of operation, business address, and phone number—which will submit corrections to fix them.

Most are fee-based services. If you're concerned about your broader digital footprint, using these services can save you an immense amount of time. There are a variety of companies providing local listings assistance, including Yext and Moz. They will identify and correct this misinformation without tedious intervention.

Resource: www.yext.com
Resource: www.moz.com/local

Yext released a 2013 study that found 43 percent of businesses had at least one incorrect or missing address in online listings.

If you're not convinced that a subscription to a service like Yext or Moz Local is right for you, you can also of course update your information the old-fashioned way with a bit of elbow grease. Below is a summary of where you go to claim your business listings, update the information that's listed there, and confirm they have all the current information.

Claim Your Space

. . . .

Site: Angie's List
How to Claim Your Listing: Register at business.angieslist.com/Registration/
SimpleRegistration.aspx
How to Update Listing Information: Sign up for a free or paid account to update your listing.

. . . .

Site: Avvo
How to Claim Your Listing: Claim your profile at www.avvo.com/claim-your-profile
How to Update Listing Information:
  1. Sign in to your Avvo account by following this link: www.avvo.com/account/login
  2. Click on the upside-down triangle next your name on the upper right-hand corner.
  3. Go to "My Avvo."
  4. Click on "Profile" in your taskbar.
  5. Once at your profile, click the "Edit My Profile" tab listed under your name.

. . . .

Site: Citysearch
How to Claim Your Listing: If your business is already listed on Citysearch and you want to claim your listing in order to make edits to it, go to signup.citygrid.com/cyb/find_business.
How to Update Listing Information: You must email Citysearch at myaccount@
citygridmedia.com.

. . . .

Site: DealerRater
How to Claim Your Listing: Claim your listing by registering at www.dealerrater.com. Then update your listing after claiming your dealership.
How to Update Listing Information: Update listing after claiming the dealership on the site.

. . . .

Site: Foursquare
How to Claim Your Listing: Claim your profile at business.foursquare.com/claim.
How to Update Listing Information: As a manager of your FourSquare listing, you can edit your listing's details, including your name, address, hours of operation, phone number, and website.

To edit your listing info, register your business with FourSquare. This will take you to your Manager Home page.

Once on this page, your first step is to select which locations you would like to edit. You can edit your info for a single location or for all of your locations at once, and create groups. By default, this page controls all locations—any changes you make will affect all of your locations.

To edit the information for your brand page and all locations (including your banner image, business description, profile photo, etc.), click on the "Listings" link under "Manage Your Locations."

. . . .

Site: Google My Business
How to Claim Your Listing: 1. Add or claim your business 2. Complete business at verification
How to Update Listing Information: support.google.com/business/answer/2911778?hl=en

. . . .

Site: Healthgrades
How to Claim Your Listing: As a health professional, you can claim your Healthgrades profile and add basic information by updating your profile at update.healthgrades.com.
How to Update Listing Information:
1. Go to update.healthgrades.com
2. Register to update your profile.
3. Enter your information.
4. Create a password.
5. Agree to the user agreement and register.

Site: TripAdvisor
How to Claim Your Listing: Before you request a listing, go to www.TripAdvisor.com/owners to make certain that a traveler hasn't already added your business to TripAdvisor. Look for the list of categories under the "Start here if you own or manage" header, select your property type, and enter your property's name.

If a match appears in the search box, click "Search," and on the next screen check that the property name and region matches. Then select "Register my business" to confirm you are affiliated with the property. If your business is already listed, you should register for the existing listing instead of creating a new one. TripAdvisor allows only one listing per property.
How to Update Listing Information: Register your business. Registering allows you to access your Management Center, where you can manage your TripAdvisor listing and reviews and correct any errors. There are also free tools to help you build your business.

Site: Vitals
How to Claim Your Listing: Visit my.vitals.com/ and click on "Claim Your Professional Profile."
How to Update Listing Information: Do this within the account interface.

Site: Yelp
How to Claim Your Listing: Go to biz.yelp.com and search for your business.
How to Update Listing Information: Sign up for a free or paid account to update your listing.

Site: ZocDoc
How to Claim Your Listing: Create the practice page at www.zocdoc.com/join
How to Update Listing Information: Submit a request to service@zocdoc.com

Site: Zomato
How to Claim Your Listing: Visit the listing for your restaurant. Click on the "Is this your business? Log in to claim it now!" link on the left navigation.
How to Update Listing Information: If a listing has incorrect information, such as a wrong address or web link, or needs to be updated with new information (like hours), click "Edit Information" to access the corrections form. Complete that form, then click "Report." Zomato will then review these changes.

8

Good, Bad, or Ugly, Make Every Review Count

• •

Jay Baer, best-selling author of *The NOW Revolution* and *Youtility*, conducted an exhaustive research study in partnership with Edison Research into the science of online complaining—who does it, why they do it, and what it all means for the business involved.

According to Baer's research, only 41 percent of people who complain on social media and rating-and-review sites expect any response from the company they're complaining about. But those who do hear back are more likely to recommend the company after the interaction because they didn't expect a response in the first place.

In this chapter, you'll learn:

✔ How to respond to various types of reviews, from scathing to glowing

✔ Why responding to as many reviews as possible is essential to your business

✔ How you can use feedback from reviews to improve your service overall

In other words, the simple dignity of a response to a complaint doubles your odds of a complainer becoming an *advocate* for your business.

This evidence speaks to the power of being an active participant in online ratings and reviews about your business. At the same time, it goes without saying that the actual response you craft is as important as the act of responding itself.

Active participation in your online ratings and reviews is essential to your bottom line. So make your ratings and reviews work for you. When it comes to negative comments, leverage them to broadcast your eagerness to listen to your customers and meet their needs. And use the positive comments to publicize your desire to maintain top-dog status.

This chapter is about how to respond to all types of reviews, whether they frame your business in a good, bad, or ugly light. There are three key parts to this chapter:

- How to handle negative reviews
- How to handle positive reviews
- When do you find time to respond?

By the end of this chapter, you'll realize that all reviews can be used to your advantage, even the negative ones. Rather than fearing them, you'll learn how to turn them into opportunities to build your business.

How to Handle Negative Reviews

General Principles

Responding to negative ratings and reviews is part art, part science. Identifying where they are, who wrote them, and what they said is the scientific bit; how you respond to such reviews is the art form. Keep the following principles in mind to master the art of responding to negative reviews:

1. **Keep calm and carry on.** Immediately repeat this mantra when you come across an unflattering review. I know your first instinct may be everything but calm—fearful, anxious,

angry, hostile, vengeful, and the like. But know that these responses won't help matters, nor are they even necessary. Remember, there's opportunity in crisis and you're going to learn how you can turn things around.

2. **Do not make it personal.** The following is an important rule of thumb, courtesy of the team at Angie's List:

Attack the issue, not the member.

Focusing on the comment, not the reviewer, keeps the conversation away from the danger zone of personal attacks. Avoid the perception of a customer versus business battle because oftentimes observers perceive the customer as the underdog being wronged by a more powerful business.

3. **Let exaggerations and hyperbole speak for themselves.** Some reviewers use flowery language in their reviews. Their dramatic tone, often intended to provoke attention, may result in anger and frustration on your part. Rather than giving more power to extreme comments, sometimes it's more effective to let these words speak for themselves. Keep in mind that other consumers—especially reasonable ones whom you want to attract—are likely to see through a hyperbolic review as over the top. Most will dismiss the review as exaggerated, assume it was written by a Socialite or Sniper, and leave with a negative impression of the reviewer, not your business.

4. **Acknowledge the reviewer's feelings.** You'd be surprised how far acknowledging someone's feelings can get you. Some people, especially Regulars or Desperate Outcriers, just want to feel heard. Without rehashing the details of a negative review, try to acknowledge the general feeling of the reviewer's experience. Utilize relatively neutral terms like "disappointed" or "not as expected." Even more neutral than this is to simply thank the reviewer. This shows readers that your business cares about its customers by listening to them and understanding their experiences. It makes your customers feel validated and not brushed off, and this alone

may de-escalate them or even convert them to a fan based on how you react to their comments.

5. **Express a proactive response.** Reach out to customers in your response by asking them to contact you so you can address their concerns in more detail. Or better yet, outline some things your business has done to rectify a complaint. For instance: Did you review the situation with your team? Did you implement new policy? This shows customers that you take them seriously. It also allows you to tell readers about an upgrade or improvement to your business.

Stop, Drop, and Roll: Your Guide to Controlling Your Responses to Negative Reviews

Wade Lombard, owner of Square Cow Movers in Austin, Texas, knows a thing or two about negative reviews. Moving is a personal business. After all, it requires uprooting a person's life. It creates an environment for potentially negative reviews—ones that sprout up even in the midst of generally good service. Over the years, his moving company has experienced the ups and downs of rating-and-review sites. Experience has provided him valuable insight into leveraging online ratings and reviews.

When a negative review shows up, Wade encourages business owners to do everything they can to avoid what he calls the *Double D: Defense and Denial*. Responding using the Double D makes your business appear unsympathetic to your customers and not open to constructive feedback.

If a customer has a valid complaint, Lombard believes it best to confront the complaint without emotion and address what's gone wrong. In his business, he avoids the Double D by following an approach he calls *Stop, Drop, and Roll*:

- **Stop** yourself from the urge to respond immediately. In other words, pause and take a break.
- **Drop** your urge to be prideful or harsh. (Remember the *Manipurated* Code of Conduct, item three: *I pledge to avoid taking reviews personally.*)
- **Roll** with the punches. Not every review is going to be perfect.

The Perfect Review Sandwich

Lombard's suggestion that you resist the urge to immediately respond to a bad review may seem like a terrible idea. But studies about how consumers interpret negative ratings and reviews support his approach.

Panagiotis Ipeirotis, an associate professor at New York University's Stern School of Business, discovered in a study that the presence of negative reviews helps bolster the validity of the positive reviews around it. In other words, negative reviews reinforce the power of the positive reviews.

Consider this a Perfect Review Sandwich:

Great Review
Great Review
Amazing Review
OK Review
Bad Review
OK Review
Great Review
Great Review

In this list, which review sticks out to you? As a business owner, your attention likely goes straight to the bad review, as if it were blazing in neon. However, you'll be surprised to learn that consumers see it very differently.

According to Professor Ipeirotis's research, consumers see the larger context of a bad review among many good ones—the proverbial forest for the tree. Rather than interpreting the single review as a mark against your business, consumers see the occasional bad review as a sign of the way the Internet works.

This means customers don't always dwell on negative reviews in the way you as a business owner may. They reference them to set the context for the positive reviews. Without negative reviews, what else is there to validate all of the good things that are said?

Imagine the perfect BLT sandwich. If you removed the bacon, you're not left with a very convincing or honest bacon, lettuce, and tomato sandwich. The same goes if you removed the negative comments from your reviews.

Most reasonable people know that even excellent businesses are bound to have things go not so perfectly once in a while. They also know that there are some unstable and impossible-to-please customers like Snipers.

So remember—as a business owner, it's natural to be horrified by a negative review and convinced that this will lead to the demise of your business. But don't panic! As this study shows, having that rare bad review actually makes your business appear genuinely good. Without it, your profile can seem kind of fishy.

How to Handle Positive Reviews

General Principles

It's an awesome feeling when a customer acknowledges the hard work and great results of your business. You may feel that the good review is a reward in itself—and it is! It's something to feel very proud of. But don't rest on your laurels just yet. There are ways to leverage good reviews so that you can extract even more than just the feelings of satisfaction. These are ways that you can turn a positive review into a gift that keeps on giving:

1. **Thank the reviewer.** Just as in person, when you receive a compliment online, you should say thank you. This shows readers that you listen to them and appreciate their business, and it encourages them to share their positive feelings about your business elsewhere.

2. **Show it off.** As you'll read in Chapter 9, share this badge of honor with the world. A positive review is an endorsement of your business and you want everyone to know about it.

3. **Highlight your good features.** If there were specific comments about aspects of your business in the review that you'd like to draw attention to, mention it in your response. For example, if someone gushes over your new pasta dish, in your response make sure you mention the months of effort that went into developing it. This is your chance to highlight

the behind-the-scenes hard work or other features that customers may not know about.

4. **Ask for referrals.** If you've created fans of your business, it doesn't hurt to gently remind them that referrals are important to your success. This can be done unobtrusively by simply stating, "Thanks for taking the time to review us. As a small business, we appreciate your spreading the word and any referrals you can make." People generally try to be helpful, especially if they think you did a good job.

Constructive Comments Embedded in Positive Reviews

Sometimes iron fists appear in velvet gloves. Once in a while, you may receive negative feedback in an otherwise positive review. Pay particular attention to friendly suggestions that appear in four- and five-star ratings and reviews. I recommend you give these top priority because they come from reviewers who hold you in high regard.

If someone has taken the time to post a five-star rating with a glowing review *and* present suggestions for improvement, what they express could be highly insightful and valuable to your business.

When Do You Find Time to Respond?

Based on his research in *Hug Your Haters,* Baer recommends responding to every complaint, on every channel, every single time.

Many of the business owners I interviewed insisted they didn't have time for such an expansive approach. They expressed they couldn't possibly fit this mammoth task into the litany of other problems they needed to solve on a daily basis.

If this is your struggle, I urge you take a moment to consider the *Manipurated* Code of Conduct. In particular, item one:

I pledge to practice good review hygiene every day.

It's precisely because of your busy schedules that this item stands at the top of the Code of Conduct. By setting aside time every day to address online ratings and reviews, you'll avoid the stress that comes from a long list of rating-and-review tasks that will pile up over time. It also helps your business avoid potential crises that come as undetected bad reviews.

Done daily, addressing your reviews takes only a few minutes. Wait to do it weekly and your time commitment suddenly feels stretched. As I shared previously on page 55, good review hygiene is similar to solid dental hygiene. If you brush before bed every evening, your teeth will thank you, and you'll avoid the consequences of neglecting your teeth.

To make the task of effectively responding to reviews more practical, refer back to Chapter 7, where you determined the top rating-and-review sites that matter most to your business. If you have limited time, you should definitely start with that high-priority list.

Finally, in order to support your time management efforts, I've developed a *Manipurated 20-Minute Quick Start Guide* (see page 142) that will make the most out of your precious and limited time.

Addressing Past Reviews

What are you going to do with all of the old, existing reviews that you uncover in your analysis in Chapter 7? Those reviews might be weeks, months, or even years old. The customers who wrote them could be gone. Do you take the time to respond to them?

From a time management perspective, most of your energy should be focused on new reviews (as well as those that have not yet been written!), which is the focus of your new customer commitment.

You might identify a few reviews that referenced specific problems that you know you have solved. Maybe it was installing a new air conditioner to make a stuffy restaurant more comfortable and the like. If you see something that you can address, do it. Just leave a quick note to thank reviewers for their feedback and let them know that you've looked into the problem and fixed it. If you are not identifying trends that are still a problem, or see complaints that were one-time flukes, you can move past those.

Replying to a small number of these past reviews will plant the seed that you're paying attention to new reviews, and as you get involved in that content you will begin to see the fruits of your labor emerging from the trees.

An Example of How to Do It Well

Greg Mohr doesn't just enjoy the gondola business. It's part of his identity. In fact, his nickname, online and offline, is Gondola Greg. Greg is the face of the gondola tours business in the United States. He is the president of the Gondola Society of America and has been known to help start-up gondola companies get their business going. He's the father figure of a very tight-knit industry in the U.S.

Greg is owner of Gondola Adventures, Inc., headquartered in Newport Beach, California. The company also has locations in Lake Las Vegas, Nevada, and Irving, Texas. As the business's name implies, it is a specialty tour operator that offers its guests highly customized cruise experiences in a luxury gondola.

Customers generally perceive that he goes the extra mile. Gondola Adventures is ranked a "Top Activity" in Newport Beach on TripAdvisor and has Yelp's coveted five-star rating.

Overall, the gondola business is not a high-volume endeavor. It's generally sought out to celebrate significant events in people's lives. According to Greg, marriage proposals and fiftieth birthdays are mainstays of his business.

Many of Greg's customers find him through rating-and-review sites. Because of the personalized nature of his product, at some point his team will have a phone conversation with customers to confirm details about the booking. From there, employees invest time learning about their guests, their needs, and the gondola experience they would like to have. And the personal nature of the relationship the company has with its customers explains why Gondola Adventure employees know the identities of most of the individuals who post reviews.

For example, some reviews mention a specific cruise date or a gondolier by name. By narrowing down the identity of nearly everyone who posts a review, Greg is able to fine-tune his customer service model in ways that are not otherwise possible.

"When we get a five-star [review], we reward the gondolier who got that five-star," he said. "And when we get something that's negative, then we want to be able to look that cruise up and figure out why it happened. . . Does that gondolier need to be given some additional training or do we need to take a look at our business protocols to make sure that a misunderstanding like that doesn't happen again?"

Whether it's glowing, terrible, or something in between, the crew at Gondola Adventures replies to most of their Yelp reviews. And they're relentless about analyzing every post. Through their consistent assessment of reviews, they've learned that even stellar five-star reviews may have some constructive comments or recommendations.

For example, in 2013, the company received a five-star review that was *nearly* entirely positive. The post ended with a short constructive comment, left in the form of a "tip."

ONE TIP- the office is hard to find. Don't go up the stairs to the address' main entrance. It's below, on left side. Gondola Adventures, please give better directions to your clients, so we won't be late!
Thanks!

Elisa Mohr, Greg's wife and business partner, warmly replied:

Thank you for your awesome review! We are happy to have provided a wonderful anniversary experience for you. We will definitely review our email and website instructions on how to find our office to make it easier for our guests to have a smooth transition from driving to sailing :-)

By taking this soft step, she ensured that the customer felt heard. The customer had already given them a five-star rating and a great review, so this extra step likely had a very positive impact.

The customer who wrote the review will be that much more likely to refer friends and families to Gondola Adventures, and to feel certain that things will go right. What's more, other customers who see that interaction on Yelp will likely feel the same way.

Now that you understand who your reviewers are, we'll explore what type of content they post. The following is a guide to diagnose reviews and craft effective responses, using a hypothetical restaurant scenario:

Response Triage Chart

· ·

Type of Review: General complaint about the business, lacks specifics
Personality: Suspicious, possibly fake
Example: *I just thought the whole experience was bad.*
What to Do: Verify if the reviewer is an actual customer. If so, explore where you may have misstepped. Address that in the review.
Example Response: *Bill, I'm very sorry to hear you were disappointed. I reviewed your experience with our team and we've addressed the* [insert issue here]. *We hope you'll give us another chance.*

If the reviewer can't be verified, post a short note on the platform (generally as a management response) apologizing and asking him to get in touch. Then provide either your phone number or email address.

· ·

Type of Review: Specific complaint about the business
Personality: Desperate Outcrier
Example: *I've eaten here so many times, and have loved it in the past. This time I tried my favorite dish, the lobster ravioli. I had to send it back, as it tasted fishy and overcooked. I felt like the server wanted to blame me for ordering the wrong dish.*
What to Do: This is an urgent one: he's a regular customer (or so he says) who has had a bad experience not only with the product but also with the staff. Verify that the lobster ravioli had an off night and seek out an answer on the service complaint ASAP.
Example Response: *Bill, I'm very sorry to hear you were disappointed. I've spoken with our kitchen team about this particular dish. Please give us a chance to make it right! We look forward to seeing you again.*

· ·

Type of Review: Constructive comment, not necessarily a complaint
Personality: The Regular
Example: *I liked the lobster ravioli, but I'd prefer more of them. I was still a bit hungry after I ate.*
What to Do: Verify that the reviewer is an actual customer. If so, review portion size. Since it was not phrased as a complaint, per se, it is your judgment call to reply to the author.
Example Response: *Bill, thanks for your comments about our award-winning lobster ravioli. We'd be happy to offer you additional ravioli in the dish next time, please don't hesitate to ask! We'd be delighted to customize this for you.*

· ·

Type of Review: Mega fan review!
Personality: The Regular
Example: *I loved the lobster ravioli so much! Can't wait to have it again.*
What to Do?: Pour yourself a celebratory beverage.
Example Response: *Thanks, Bill, for your comments! We love it too, and can't wait to see you again.*

....

Type of Review: Balanced review
Personality: The Regular
Example: *Overall it was great and I'm excited to try more of the menu. Couple of minor issues with our meal, nothing that would stop me from going back.*
What to Do: Verify that the reviewer is an actual customer. Then explore what the minor issues were, but do it offline by providing your contact information.
Example Response: *Thanks for your comments, Bill. I'm happy to hear you enjoyed your meal! Please let me know what left you disappointed and we'll address it. I can be reached at* [insert your phone number or email here].

....

Type of Review: Takedown
Personality: The Sniper
Example: *This place is terrible. Everything was awful. The tables were sticky, the food was cold and the servers were SO RUDE. I am never giving them my money AGAIN.*
What to Do: This might have been a real customer, but nothing you can say is going to have an impact. Your safest approach is to apologize and get out of the way. Chances are high you'll never hear from this customer, even when you've given contact information. Others who read the review will see the Sniper attempt but will also appreciate your response.
Example Response: *We're sorry to hear about your meal. We would like to learn more about your experience. I can be reached at* [insert your phone number or email here].

....

Type of Review: Jargony review
Personality: The Socialite
Example: ****PASTA KING HIGHLY RECOMMENDED****
Came here with DOOCHIN and WIZKID and OMG the pasta is da' bomb! I have 100 loves in this world none of them lobster but the lobster ravioli here is off da' charts! 4 Rockets on the City Top Pasta Chart.
What to Do: You may not understand everything the Socialite says, but be appreciative for the generous comments.
Example Response: *PastaKing, thanks for your review! Hope you see you again, we'll have some lobster ravioli ready for you.*

....

Type of Review: Fake review

Personality: Suspicious, fake review

Example: *I used to come here all the time and then everything changed for the worse. It caused me to look for other restaurants nearby that I can be a regular at.*

What to Do: Your suspicions are probably right here—reviews like this, and other versions of them, are quite possibly fake. Not enough detail, not enough specifics, and they're hinting at other businesses nearby. First, if it is egregious enough, flag the review on the platform. Then respond but very generally.

Example Response: *We're sorry to hear about your meal. We would like to learn more about your experience. I can be reached at* [insert your phone number or email here].

9

The Fresh Factor

In 2010, Dr. Irena Vaksman launched her San Francisco–based dental practice. From the start, she knew the Bay Area was one of the most competitive dental markets in the nation. This meant that her hunt for customers would be one of the most important things she could do to support her business.

Like so many ambitious start-up entrepreneurs, she was swamped with an endless list of to-do items. Fortunately, her husband, Robert, a successful attorney in his own right, took on the marketing efforts of her fledgling dental office. This freed Dr. Vaksman to focus on providing excellent patient service.

In this chapter, you'll learn:

✔ How freshness helps your business outmaneuver the rating-and-review platform

✔ How to generate more reviews

✔ The right way and the wrong way to seek reviews

✔ How the shifting trend toward mobile searches impacts your ratings and reviews and, ultimately, your strategy for managing them

The two decided to run a special dental checkup deal on Groupon, which itself had launched only two years earlier. Within a short period of time, their savvy marketing move paid off—more than 300 new customers signed up for the deal and her practice grew exponentially overnight.

With this newfound success there came an overwhelming responsibility to retain those customers and keep them in her practice. "We just wanted to leverage technology in any way possible to push us forward," said Robert.

San Francisco is a city filled with tech-savvy people, and Robert knew that many of their new patients who signed up on Groupon would be likely to post comments on Yelp. He recognized the high volume of new reviews would have lasting freshness benefits even after the Groupon promotion had delivered all of its customers.

"At the end of the day, we're not the only ones in the business. We have to get content up, stay ahead of the conversations, and we know all our competitors are in the same boat," said Robert.

Those 300 customers were an immediate win for Dr. Vaksman's newly built practice, but the reviews that were written early had a lasting impact on the business by boosting the practice's freshness factor. Remember: new content and reviews mean more freshness. In effect, the dental practice successfully leveraged one marketing platform (social media) to enhance another (rating-and-review).

What Freshness Means for Your Business

As you learned in Chapter 2, the speed at which their content refreshes is one of the biggest reasons rating-and-review companies have exploded onto the Internet scene and dominated search results. In fact, Yelp alone processes more than 26,000 new reviews *per minute*—that's an astounding volume of content. And you now know that Google loves fresh content. Freshness is one of the best ways to remain relevant to Google's unforgiving, secret, and ever-changing algorithms.

The sites driving customers to you depend on freshness, so you should, too. And the simplest way you can do this is by boosting new reviews. By generating new ratings and reviews about your business, you'll leverage the benefits of freshness.

How Do I Generate Fresh Content on Rating-and-Review Sites?

This chapter shows you how you can generate more ratings and reviews on your business in a way that favors your business. You'll find out who you should target when asking for a review, where to launch your efforts, and how to do it in a way that doesn't break any rules.

Target the Right People

Many business owners new to Yelp think that asking friends and family members to endorse their businesses on Yelp will boost their presence on the site. They quickly learn their efforts are usually a complete waste of time.

This is because Yelp prefers reviews posted by its most active members. Reviews Yelp receives from people it does not know (which is to say, someone who is not active on Yelp) will most likely be screened and filtered out.

The key point is knowing that when it comes to some sites—notably Yelp—not all reviewers are created equal. Some sites distinguish reviewers whom they consider more credible. Reviews submitted by these "known" reviewers are prioritized and more likely to be displayed. By the same token, some reviewers are considered by sites to be less reliable, or "unknown," so reviews submitted by these folks are likely to be filtered out.

Though it may seem like a good idea to solicit reviews from every customer at every interaction, this may turn out to be a big waste of time and effort. Rather than follow this misguided tactic (or worse yet, set out in search of fake reviews), you need to take a different approach.

One business owner in the travel and tourism industry I interviewed trained her customer-facing team to politely ask for reviews, but in a targeted and efficient way. For her, Yelp and TripAdvisor are the biggest sources of her new customers.

If a customer says to an employee, "Thank you so much! That was the best trip I've had in a long time," which is a compliment the company hears often, her team is instructed to follow this protocol:

1. Thank the customer profusely.
2. Ask, "By chance, are you on Yelp?"

If the customer answers yes, then the team member says the following:

> We'd love to hear your feedback on our Yelp page
> when you think about it.

If the customer answers no, the team member knows not to encourage that customer to post on Yelp. Instead, the employee is trained to encourage a review on a site that is likelier to post the customer's feedback by saying the following:

> We'd love to hear your feedback on our TripAdvisor page
> when you think about it.

See how that works? It's a gentle way to reinforce, at the point of transaction, the importance of soliciting online reviews from customers with impact on a particular review site. It sends the right customers down the appropriate path—one that actually stands a chance at rewarding you.

The downside is the low-volume nature of this strategy. Those conversations happen only every so often, and they cannot be relied upon alone to generate the reviews needed. That's where other tools come in.

Shoot for the Stars

You learned earlier the difference between reviews (consisting of written comments and statements) and ratings (consisting of quicker assessments such as star counts, numerical ranking, and letter grades) to reflect how good a business is.

Because reviews allow for lengthier comments, specific accounts, and personalization, most businesses and customers find that they convey more information and feedback about a business. As such, it may be tempting to simply ask customers for detailed reviews about their experience with you and overlook asking for a rating.

Key point—don't overlook the rating!

Whether it's a star rating on Yelp, a dot rating on TripAdvisor, or a letter grade on Angie's List, get in the habit of soliciting this feedback from your customers as well. These ratings require less effort and time on the part of your customers since they don't have to compose any words. And for potential customers with limited time researching your business, these ratings give them a quick gestalt of how your business stands among the heap of competitors. Finally, as you'll read in the section on how emerging mobile trends (see page 109) are shaping this field, ratings may become the primary source of information on smartphones and smart watches.

What About Facebook?

If you are a business owner who manages a Facebook page, you might have experienced the power of that medium and its billion members.

Indeed, it can be an excellent means to connect with your customers, interact with them, and keep them engaged with content from your business.

In the marketing landscape, Facebook would generally fall under the category of social media marketing. But did you know Facebook also offers ratings and reviews on its site?

If your business has a heavy emphasis on Facebook, then you might want to read on.

Facebook's rating-and-review system is cumbersome to use and is not enabled automatically for all business pages. To start, your business must be in the Local Businesses category on Facebook for ratings and reviews to even be an option. If that fits your description, follow this five-step process to enable the system:

1. Click "About" below your Page's cover photo.
2. Click "Page Info" in the left column.

3. Click to edit the "Address" section; enter your address here and click to save the change; when you do this, a map will appear in this section.

4. Click to edit the "Address" section again. Below the map, click to check the box next to "Show" map, check-ins, and star ratings on the page.

5. Save "Changes."

Those changes should enable customers to start leaving ratings and reviews on your Facebook business page. They'll do this by visiting your Facebook page and clicking on your "Reviews" tab. The star rating for your business will also now start showing as part of your Facebook page profile to other users.

Like other rating-and-review services, Facebook permits consumers to leave both star ratings and written feedback. Its system is somewhat confusing, as consumers can select specifically who can see their feedback—so if they're sharing a story they want only their friends to see, that privacy selection can be made and won't be known to you or others who view your profile.

The star ratings on Facebook are a helpful way for consumers to validate your business when they're looking for you on Facebook. But there are some inherent problems with Facebook's current rating-and-review platform that are unique to its platform that you need to know about:

1. **You don't always know who is reviewing you.** Yes, fake reviews are a problem even on Facebook. Over time you'll probably notice some reviews that look awfully suspicious— indeed, likely even fake. Beyond that, if customers have their privacy settings set to anything other than "public," you will not see their rating at all. It will only be visible to their friends.

2. **Why did they give their assigned star rating?** Part of the value of ratings and reviews is it gives you feedback about what you did right, or suggestions for what you might improve. Was something great about a customer's experience? Facebook has no requirement to fill out a review. It allows consumers to leave a star rating and move on without writing the review.

That feedback is less helpful to you, or anyone else, if it doesn't have context.

3. **Cumbersome management response.** Unlike other rating-and-review sites, Facebook has not provided an easy mechanism for businesses to respond to reviews. Facebook does permit you to "Like" the review, or to leave comments on it as you would with any other status update on Facebook. As noted above, that is all predicated on the fact that the review is visible to you in the first place.

4. **Poor analytics.** Possibly the only helpful piece of analysis that Facebook offers on its rating-and-review platform is that it orders the reviews by the star rating. Therefore, you'll see all of the five-star reviews, followed by all of the four-star reviews, and so on. Sadly, it does not further sort them by chronological order, meaning you have to pick through them to see recent reviews or look for trends. The most reliable way to track reviews on Facebook is to subscribe to a third-party tool that will give you the ability to look at reviews on Facebook in a bit more depth.

5. **Multilocation failure.** This is a serious flaw with Facebook's system, and it affects more than just ratings and reviews. Facebook has an awkward method for managing businesses that have multiple locations (say, a coffee shop with six locations in a city). Its function called Facebook Locations (previously known as Parent-Child) permits a business to link all of its locations to one single Facebook page. The challenge with doing this is it requires either a Facebook sales rep or a third-party agency to activate and request it. This is a nonstarter for the many business owners who have neither resource available to them. There are currently no work-arounds to this process. You cannot activate Facebook's rating-and-review service without an address, but you can add one address per Facebook business page.

All of this points to gaping holes in Facebook's strategy for ratings and reviews. Clearly, ratings and reviews is a big business, and I would not be surprised if Facebook comes out with a groundbreaking new rating-and-review offering that trumps offerings from Yelp and others.

Until that happens, Facebook's current effort will be frustrating for business owners to use. Nevertheless, if Facebook represents a big part of your customer connection, you should consider activating and encouraging reviews on the platform. Follow the same advice for soliciting those reviews as I've recommended for other sites.

If you want to explore the Facebook Locations framework, you'll need to seek out one of their Facebook Marketing Partners.

Resource: www.facebookmarketingpartners.com

Email

Not all businesses maintain an email database, but if you do, know that your email database is a powerful tool to harvest reviews—but only if you do it properly.

If you send an email, out of the blue, to your customer email list that says "Review us on Angie's List!" your customers are likely to see this as a bit intrusive—"Why here, and why now?" There is no context to the communication. It might have been weeks or months, or longer, since they had a transaction with you. Details won't be fresh in their mind, and few customers will probably take the step to write a review solicited in this manner. Further, openly asking for reviews this way may violate the rating-and-review site terms of use.

But you can encourage reviews by adding links to your rating-and-review sites in every single email you send. For instance, think about this when sending out an email blast to promote a new product or service, to update information about your business, or to remind customers about routine follow-up and maintenance appointments.

The method you use to do this is up to you. You can include it as a sentence in the copy with a hyperlink to your page, or use a graphic or image. But it reinforces to the customer that you're on those sites, and that alone may generate reviews.

Offline Tips: Storefront Signs and Business Cards

By posting a "We're on Yelp" and "We're on TripAdvisor" sign on your front door, you're telling your customers, "We're listening and want your feedback. Can you help us out?"

Most of the big review platforms will send you free stickers to put on your window, which is a far better idea than making a possibly unprofessional-looking homemade sign on your color printer.

Where to Obtain Window Clings and Stickers

Yelp: www.manipurated.com/YelpSticker

TripAdvisor: www.manipurated.com/TripAdvisorSticker

Angie's List: www.manipurated.com/AngiesListSticker

DealerRater: www.manipurated.com/DealerRaterSticker

As far as your business cards are concerned, consider including the logo of your top online rating-and-review sites. Keep in mind, each platform has its own brand usage guidelines. Many prohibit language that outright prompts a person to post a review.

This means you should restrain yourself from the urge to run out and print a bunch of business cards that say "Review us on [insert rating-and-review site here]" and "Give us five stars on [insert rating-and-review site here]."

On the other hand, you can safely say, "We're on [insert rating-and-review site here]," and let the customer figure out the rest.

Measuring Up: Rating-and-Review Sites Rules

The following chart summarizes the current rules regarding the solicitation of reviews. Remember, violating these rules can earn you a permanent electronic scarlet letter on your rating-and-review profile that your online prospects and customers will see.

Site	Is It OK to Solicit Reviews?	Link for Further Information
Angie's List	Yes. The company also offers a tool called Fetch to help businesses generate more reviews.	support.business.angieslist.com/app/answers/detail/a_id/172/related/1
Avvo	No policy against it	
Citysearch	No policy against it	
DealerRater	Yes	blog.dealerrater.com/how-does-your-dealership-get-more-reviews
Facebook	No policy against it	
Foursquare	No policy against it	
Google My Business	Yes, phrased as "leave feedback on Google"	support.google.com/business/answer/3474122?hl=en
Healthgrades	No policy against it	
TripAdvisor	Yes	www.tripadvisor.com/TripAdvisorInsights/n2319/6-ways-generate-more-positive-reviews
Vitals	Policy unclear	
Yelp	Never OK	biz.yelp.com/support/review_solicitation
ZocDoc	Policy unclear	blog.zocdoc.com/verified-reviews-why-they-work/
Zomato	Never OK	www.zomato.com/policies

Soliciting Reviews from Major Review Sites

So what's the difference between soliciting reviews and asking for feedback? As you can see, policies from even the rating-and-review sites themselves can be unclear. To avoid experiencing the wrath from sites for breaking their rules, I recommend you practice caution. As a rule of thumb, the safest route is to simply tell your customers which rating-and-review sites you're on and say you always appreciate their feedback and help.

Impacts of Shifting to Mobile

According to an eMarketer study, by the end of 2015, consumer mobile searches will make up 70 percent of all Google search activity.[1] In other words, almost three-quarters of the search traffic on the world's largest and most powerful search engine will be coming from mobile devices.

So how does this impact your business?

There are two ways: Mobilegeddon and Star Ratings.

First, Google updated its computer algorithms in early 2015. That update, dubbed "mobilegeddon" by the technology industry, set forth new parameters regarding how Google prefers a website to function.

Because an increasing majority of its customers are searching with mobile devices, Google wants all websites to have a mobile-friendly interface. This means you basically have two versions of your website: a version that shows up on desktop computers one way, and a version that shows up on mobile devices (such as tablets and smartphones) another way. Some sites use so-called responsive design, meaning a single website conforms itself to various display sizes automatically.

Sites that don't comply with this new mobile-friendly mandate will be penalized in Google's search results. If you're not sure about your site's status, Google released a helpful tool that confirms how the company sees your website and provides recommendations for optimizing your site for mobile:

Resource: www.google.com/
webmasters/tools/mobile-friendly/

Google will confirm for you what it sees when it computers visit your site. If Google doesn't feel that you comply with the new mandate, it will provide you with instructions to bring your site up to the mobile standard.

1 www.slideshare.net/eMarketerInc/e-marketer-webinarkeydigitaltrends15thi ngsknow2015

That's the first and most immediate way mobile search impacts your business. The second way it impacts your business is a bit more complicated. It turns out consumers use online rating-and-review sites differently on mobile devices than they do on desktop computers. This follows a general trend of how consumers interact with the Internet on mobile devices versus desktop computers. The marketing and technology industries refer to these differences as **site usability**—how people use a technology and what they do with it.

As far as mobile devices are concerned, their screens are much smaller than those of desktop computers, and they're generally used while people are away from their computer. Therefore, the average consumer's mobile use is framed by convenience and speed. Consumers ask themselves, "Is the site easy to navigate?" and "Can I do what I need quickly and with a minimum of clicks?" These aren't new questions, but the limitations of small screens have heightened their importance.

On Yelp, for example, a consumer on a desktop computer may pay equal attention to a business's star ratings and reviews. On a mobile device, that same consumer is likely to be more focused on the star ratings than on reviews, and he or she certainly won't be as likely to scroll through more than a handful of reviews. This is because Yelp's mobile version dramatically reduces the amount of screen real estate it allocates for written reviews. Whereas you'll see a total-review count next to your star rating, you may only see a fraction of the first sentence of a small number of actual reviews. Many consumers won't make the effort required to read entire reviews.

Review authors have wisened up to this trend, and you'll notice some include a review summary at the top of their review. Those review authors are battling the same trend you are, and they're still fishing for the FUC'd (Funny, Useful, Cool) votes, even on a mobile device.

Smaller Than Smartphones

If a smartphone's diminutive screen has altered the way consumers interact with online ratings and reviews, consider the impact of wearable devices such as the Apple Watch. Now, screens become even smaller. For example, to read a review on the Apple Watch, you have to click through several screens to access it. It takes a lot of tapping to read a single review.

Imagine it's noontime. A hungry consumer is walking outside, staring at her Apple Watch, looking for a good place to grab lunch. Do you think she'll bother reading lengthy reviews and management responses from her watch's tiny screen? Probably not. Instead, she'll focus only on the star ratings.

Nearly three-quarters of all consumers conduct pre-purchase research on their mobile devices. So as screens go mobile and become even smaller, you're charged with placing even more emphasis on capturing star ratings that reflect your business accurately—those stars may be the sole initial criterion your prospects use to find you.

Again, think freshness. The way to combat lower star ratings is to fix what people report to be broken or disappointing about your business and to boost the stars you receive through new ratings and reviews. These are ways to make the rating-and-review sites work harder for you. The good news is if your business is short on stars, a single review can improve your overall rating dramatically.

The Review Funnel

Previously, you learned about the fake review industry. Business owners sometimes turn to this dark side of the rating-and-review world in an effort to boost freshness.

There are also legitimate companies that help business owners increase their ratings and reviews by making it easier for the consumer to write and submit reviews. Their above-board tactics are permissible and sometimes even recommended by the major rating-and-review sites.

This line of logic is generally called a *review funnel*. Many companies are providing these services, some in very specialized categories. Grade.us and CrowdTempo are two of the larger such companies.

> Resource: www.grade.us
> Resource: www.crowdtempo.com

Review funnel providers offer automated tools that allow you to ask for and remind your customers to post ratings and reviews on the sites you specify. However, rather than having to visit individual rating-and-review sites one by one (which few customers are likely to do), your customers use a review portal set up by the funnel provider. There, they can review your business. Their review will then be submitted to your desired rating-and-review sites in each site's appropriate format.

By funneling reviews this way, these companies can help you amplify one customer review onto multiple sites of your choosing. In other words, it can multiply freshness.

Also, because reviewers submit reviews to these companies instead of rating-and-review sites, some even allow you to intercept angry reviews before they're published. Reviewers are first directed to the business for acknowledgment and resolution before the review is submitted to the rating-and-review platform.

You've learned how important fresh reviews are to the sites where they're hosted, and also why they're good for your business. With the tips in this chapter, you'll be on the way to generating new reviews regularly and keeping the stream of fresh content flowing.

Is It Possible to Overcome Yelp's Review Filter?

I'd like to address one of the most common complaints business owners have about Yelp's system: "I have lots of four- and five-star ratings on Yelp. Why aren't they showing up?"

If you're not familiar with Yelp's filter and algorithm, their proprietary system automatically filters some reviews—in some cases a high percentage of your reviews—out of public view to an area it calls "reviews that are not currently recommended." These are not factored into a business's overall star rating and are not shown on the main reviews page for the business.

Is it possible to get past Yelp's filter and move those reviews back to your business's profile?

Maybe, but not in any official way. The following is one work-around that has proved successful for many business owners. With that said, this approach may not work for you and it may also irritate Yelp, the equivalent of "poking the bear." Proceed at your own caution, as these directions are intended for people with advanced Internet skills:

1. If you don't already have one, set up a Yelp account.
2. Make sure you remain logged in throughout this process.
3. Once you're on your business's Yelp profile page, find the area containing "reviews that are not currently recommended" for your business. This is a small gray link at the bottom of your list of reviews.
4. Look through the reviews here. See some that you feel should be promoted or moved onto your profile page?

You want to focus on reviews that appear very legitimate and you know haven't been purchased or written by friends and family. Also, focus on reviews posted by Yelpers who have high numbers of friends and reviews (you may likely see many profiles with *0 Friends* and low review counts; ignore these Yelpers because Yelp is unlikely to show their reviews). You're going to want to "Follow" this list of Yelpers using the process below.

5. The next step requires you to view that Yelper's profile. You can't do this on the current page you're on. In order to view a Yelper's profile, make a note of the reviewer's name and city.

6. Open a new window in your web browser. Find the Yelper through a Google search by typing the following:
   a. Yelp [insert Yelper name here] [insert city here]
   b. Often, the Yelper's profile will appear in Google's search results. If so, click on that link and proceed to the next step.

7. Once you're on the Yelper's profile page, navigate on the left column and find "Follow This Reviewer" and select this option.

8. You're done. Your endorsement of the Yelper may be enough to elevate his or her reviews. Results may not be immediate, but if it works you've helped promote both the Yelper (good for their visibility) and his or her review of your business. It's a win-win.

Last, if customers mention that they wrote you a great Yelp review that never appeared, you can ask them to do the following to get them more active on Yelp's system and possibly elevate their status in the eyes of Yelp's algorithm:

- Add a profile image to their profile.
- Regularly "check in" on Yelp when they visit new places, including yours.

- Write Yelp reviews for other places they frequent—this gets them more active on the Yelp site.

Disclaimer: Do not use any of these tips to promote posts from friends and family or fake reviews. Doing so will put your profile at extreme risk.

10

Be a Peacock: Boldly Show Your Feathers

Think about the reason you picked up this book: it probably had to do, at least in part, with a negative experience with ratings and reviews. Too much of a business owner's experience is steeped in that type of experience—you're fed up, frustrated, and ready to throw in the gloves on all of it.

No doubt there is plenty to be frustrated about, and none of this is easy stuff.

But there is a positive side to online reviews. When a customer leaves you a glowing review, one that highlights all the best aspects of your business, it's a wonderful feeling.

In this chapter, you'll learn:

✔ Why you should think about showing off your positive reviews

✔ Where you should consider featuring your testimonials and good reviews

✔ What sites offer awards or honors to businesses, and how you qualify and apply for them

You did great. You earned it, and you deserve it! It demonstrates you're doing something, likely *many* things, right. You're listening to your customers. You're being responsive to them. And they've noticed. You should proudly showcase all of your effort.

There are two reasons to show off your positive reviews and awards: new customers and existing customers. Prospective customers of your business turn to rating-and-review sites as a primary online source of information when they're making a purchase decision. This reinforces what you've known on a gut level all along: *most people care about what others think.*

What you might not have suspected, though, is that positive reviews and awards can also sway and influence your existing fans and customers. These individuals want to know someone else loves the business they frequent just as much as they do.

After all, who doesn't enjoy being in good company? In other words, nothing validates a person's positive opinion of your business quite like another equally happy customer. People like to organize into tribes.

Therefore, when it comes to showing off your positive ratings and reviews to the world, you're presented with a double-rainbow opportunity. Consider this a two-for-one online deal: First, you influence your prospective customers. Second, you impress your existing ones. How great is that combination?

Where to Promote Your Ratings and Reviews

You will come across compelling ratings and reviews that you want to share with the world. Perhaps a customer who had such an exceptional experience with your business that you cannot wait to tell others about it.

You can promote these positive reviews, but first you need to determine where you'll take that action. The "where" is called a *venue*. The venue can vary depending on your needs and circumstances. The primary venues are through your website, email, and social media.

Your Website

This is an effective venue to promote quotes from your best hand-picked online reviews. Each site has different rules about how to do this, but most provide a convenient piece of very simple website code (called an *HTML embed code*) that you will cut and paste onto your website. Most major rating-and-review sites prefer you use their embed capabilities rather than copy and paste the review.

During a National Public Radio interview, Vince Sollitto, Yelp's vice president of Global Corporate Communications and Government Relations, answered questions from small business owners. One woman asked why some great reviews were filtered out of her Yelp profile while negative reviews remained. She said she had one negative review showing on her page while forty positive reviews remained hidden.

"Your website is the perfect place to post those [positive reviews]. Our website is where we post review content that we know, and we have enough confidence in to trust and provide to customers," Sollito said.

If an executive from Yelp thinks it's a good idea to post flattering reviews on your site, maybe you should, too. So how do you go about accomplishing this task?

How to Embed Reviews on Your Website

The method of displaying a review on your own website is generally achieved through the use of a technology called a *widget*. What's a widget?

Generally speaking, widgets are simple framed objects that you can embed on your website simply by copying and pasting a few lines of HTML code. It requires a little bit of technical knowledge, but the rating-and-review sites will give you all of the widget code (almost always for free), and most have different sizes and shapes to suit the design of your website. For instance, TripAdvisor has a whole page of free widgets available to property and restaurant owners that will automatically display things like recent reviews, current star ratings, a small TripAdvisor button, and so on. Figure 10.1 is an example a one of TripAdvisor's widgets.

Figure 10.1. TripAdvisor Widget

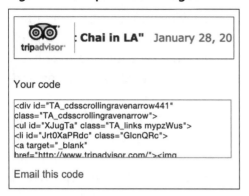

Your code

```
<div id="TA_cdsscrollingravenarrow441"
class="TA_cdsscrollingravenarrow">
<ul id="XJugTa" class="TA_links mypzWus">
<li id="Jrt0XaPRdc" class="GlcnQRc">
<a target="_blank"
href="http://www.tripadvisor.com/"><img
```

Email this code

Embed Codes for Popular Sites

Not all of the top fifteen rating-and-review sites provide these widgets, so if a particular website does not appear in the list below, it does not currently have widget tools available.

Site	What's Available	Link
Angie's List	A free customized badge to use on your website	www.angieslist.com/angie-badge/
Avvo	A variety of widgets you can embed on your website.	www.avvo.com/partner_with_us/widgets
DealerRater	A large number of tools and widgets available to its dealer partners.	Inquire about the Certified DealerRater program.
Healthgrades	No widgets you can embed on your website	n/a
Yelp	A simple widget to embed recent Yelp reviews on your website.	www.yelp.com/bling
TripAdvisor	Depending on your business, a variety of widgets you can embed on your website. Follow the link to the TripAdvisor site to see what is available.	www.tripadvisor.com/Widgets

Native Reviews on Your Website

Another option is to capture your own reviews, skipping major rating-and-review sites altogether. I call these *native reviews*, as they live "natively" on your website. They're captured on your website, hosted on your website, and managed by you, not a third-party rating-and-review site.

This option works well if you have a large amount of monthly site traffic, tend to have a lot of descriptions about product and services that you offer on your website (thereby giving a visitor a number of things to actually review), and have the technical expertise to implement the technology.

There are a few major benefits to hosting your own reviews on your website:

1. It allows you to moderate the reviews (you're in control, after all, and you can remove reviews).
2. Just as lots of fresh reviews ensure Yelp's freshness in Google's algorithm, fresh reviews on your own website have the same positive effect.
3. Allowing customers the opportunity to give you feedback on your website that is then featured tells customers that you really do take their feedback seriously, particularly if you practice restraint and allow some negative or critical reviews in the mix (remember the Perfect Review Sandwich).
4. Unlike a review on Yelp or Angie's List, reviews on your own website may help a prospective customer make a smarter choice about what they may want or need from you, as the reviews give them real-time context.

If you've determined native reviews are something you want to explore, consider one of the two tools listed in the adjacent table for your website. None of them require extensive technical knowledge or a complete website redesign.

Software Name	Description	Links and Further Information
WP Customer Reviews	Free tool for WordPress websites that enables you to capture customer reviews on your website. Reviews are designed to be readable by Google.	wordpress.org/plugins/wp-customer-reviews
ReVu	This software enables reviews and can be embedded on most website hosting services. Also available as a WordPress plug-in.	www.re-vu.com

Email

Consider allocating space in your customer email to thank a customer for a recent review, address a request or complaint (particularly when you've worked hard to resolve it), or feature a customer of the month. In general, you will always want to receive permission from the person who wrote the review.

How might you feature reviews in an email?

You might do a customer of the month campaign highlighting a photo and a brief testimonial, with a link to the rating-and-review platform where the customer wrote the review. If you have the capability, you can also consider shooting a short video with your phone, provided the quality is acceptable.

Figure 10.2 gives an example of how one company includes reviews in its email. This email is from Embrace Pet Insurance, which provides pet health insurance. The company includes reviews in its email from a pet insurance review site (talk about a specialty review site; imagine what their top priority list looks like!).

Figure 10.2. Reviews in email

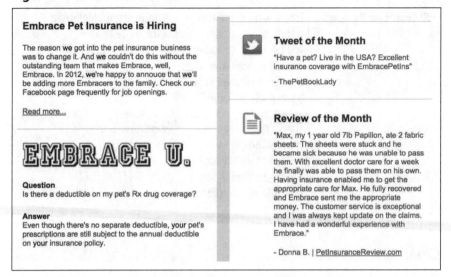

Social Media

Your existing social media channels, such as Twitter and Facebook, are important places to link to a review. In your posts, describe what excited you about a particular customer's experience, what you've learned from it, or why it's important to you. You might highlight a review of a new service you've just launched, or a new item you just added to the menu. It's a great way to showcase that you are listening to your customers and to show off the good things customers have to say about you. In essence, this allows you to leverage a single review from one platform (rating-and-review) to another platform (social media).

Many of the top rating-and-review sites do not make it easy to find the permanent link to a specific review (Yelp in particular, although I have included a work-around below). If you find you

> **How to Obtain the Direct Link on Yelp:** Hover your mouse cursor over the review you'd like to share, and on the left side of the review a link to four options will appear. Click on "Share Review" and then copy the link from the box directly under the Facebook and Twitter logos.

cannot locate such a link, simply mention the review and thank the reviewer for his or her contribution.

Awards

Most of the top rating-and-review sites have developed programs that recognize business owners for their online accomplishments. You might have been notified about such an award by mail or email or by logging in to the rating-and-review site.

These awards are an excellent credential, particularly if you've received the award from one of your top rating-and-review sites identified in Chapter 7. It is an immediate credential that says to prospective and current customers: "I'm legit."

You will want to feature these awards in your email, on your website, and even physically in your place of business. Many of the platforms will send you physical badges, window clings, and other promotional items that allow you to easily show off how active you are on a particular rating-and-review site.

The following is a roundup of the most common accolades from the top fifteen rating-and-review sites. In addition to these, you may occasionally receive specialty awards that are not detailed here (like "Business of the Year," for example). For most of these, no application or submission is necessary.

Awards and Honors

- -

Site: Angie's List
Description: The Angie's List Super Service Award criteria are complex. In addition to maintaining a high rating (3.5 or higher), Angie's List must be active in your city for at least one year. Background checks are also required. The program period is October 31 to November 1 of the following year.
Link: support.business.angieslist.com/app/answers/detail/a_id/121/~/the-angies-list-super-service-award---eligibility

....

Site: Avvo
Description: Avvo's awards program is pretty straightforward. You determine your eligibility for all of its awards by logging in to your Avvo account. From there, you'll see which awards and badges are available to you.
Link: Additional information is available within the Avvo lawyer dashboard.

....

Site: Citysearch
Description: Best of Citysearch is a vote-driven program. A Citysearch panel determines eligibility, and the business finalists are then voted on by the Citysearch community.
Link: www.citysearch.com/best

Site: DealerRater
Description: Two options available to members of the Certified Dealers Program.

    1. Dealer of the Year (DOTY): This program recognizes a select number of car dealerships throughout the United States and Canada for outstanding customer satisfaction. DealerRater awards recipients based on online reviews posted on its site.

    2. Consumer Satisfaction Awards (CSA): Unveiled in 2015, these awards are an expansion of DealerRater's annual recognition program that recognizes top car dealerships in the United States and Canada.

      In order to be eligible for the DealerRater Consumer Satisfaction Awards, dealerships must meet the requirements that the company puts forth for the Dealer of the Year Program—most recently, to have at least twenty-five reviews, an average consumer rating of 4.0 out of 5.0, and a minimum of one review per quarter. These requirements applied to the 2014 awards and may be subject to change in future years.
Link: www.dealerrater.com/cdp/default.aspx

Site: Healthgrades
Description: Healthgrades maintains four award programs:

    1. Outstanding Patient Experience Award
    2. Patient Safety Excellence Award
    3. America's Best Hospitals™
    4. Distinguished Hospital Award for Clinical Excellence™
Link: Contact Healthgrades for further information.

Site: TripAdvisor
Description: TripAdvisor currently has three award programs for businesses.

    1. Travelers' Choice Awards: These are the highest honor TripAdvisor bestows. They are based on millions of reviews and opinions from travelers around the world. These annual awards reflect "the best of the best." Hotels and other accommodations, destinations, attractions, brands, and products are judged for service, quality, and customer satisfaction.

    2. Certificate of Excellence : This award honors accommodations, attractions, and restaurants that consistently demonstrate a commitment to hospitality excellence. To be eligible, a business must maintain an overall rating of four or higher (out of five) from travelers on TripAdvisor. Additional criteria include the volume of reviews received within the last twelve months.

3. GreenLeader: This program recognizes hotels and bed-and-breakfasts that engage in environmentally friendly practices. The objective is to make it easier for travelers to find and book a greener stay. TripAdvisor grants the award on a rolling basis based on applications hotels submit. Qualifying properties are marked with a badge on their TripAdvisor page. Attractions and restaurants are not eligible for GreenLeader awards.
Link: www.tripadvisorsupport.com/hc/en-us/articles/200614097

....

Site: Yelp
Description: Yelp has a popular "People Love Us On Yelp" window cling. Yelp's materials are sent automatically to qualifying businesses twice annually. Criteria for inclusion are not disclosed.
Link: www.yelp-support.com/article/How-do-I-get-a-People-Love-Us-on-Yelp-window-cling-for-my-business?l=en_US

....

Site: ZocDocs
Description:

    1. Rapid Registration: Doctors with this icon on their profile have provided digital forms for ZocDoc patients to fill out before arriving at the office. Patients can both fill out and submit these forms on ZocDoc's useful feature, ZocDoc Check-In.

    2. Scheduling Hero: This award recognizes doctor's offices that maintain up-to-date lists of insurance programs they accept and that are noted for doing an excellent job with keeping to their schedule. It is based on patient feedback.

    3. See You Again: This is an award to doctors who receive a large number of ZocDoc patients who book repeatedly with them. This award demonstrates that these offices excel at cultivating strong, long-lasting relationships with their patients.

    4. Speedy Response: Offices who've earned this award consistently confirm patient appointment requests on ZocDoc within one business hour. With these award winners, patients can be extra sure that their last-minute appointments will be honored.
Link: blog.zocdoc.com/zocdoc-our-team-blog-and-the-award-goes-to

....

As you can see, you have many ways to promote your ratings, reviews, and accolades. Taking a comprehensive approach to showcasing them ensures that customers—both prospective and existing—have a full, complete, and accurate picture of how fabulous your business actually is.

11

Seeking a Higher Power

• •

Carol Neumann owns and manages Dancing Deer Mountain, a facility that hosts weddings. The event center is located in Junction City, Oregon, and provides couples an idyllic Pacific Northwest setting for their big day.

Dancing Deer Mountain books weddings from May to October and closes during the cold winter months. A few days after hosting a wedding in 2011, Neumann checked her business's Google reviews and noticed a review from Christopher Liles, the bride's brother-in-law.

In his review, Liles said

In this chapter, you'll learn:

✔ How to flag problematic reviews

✔ How sites evaluate requests to remove posts or act on flag requests

✔ How to assess the trustworthiness of outside reputation management firms

✔ When and how to seek legal help

Dancing Deer Mountain was "the worst experience of my life." He described one of the buildings on the property as a "tool shed that was painted pretty, but a tool shed all the same."

Neumann disagreed with the assessment of her wedding facility. In fact, she thought it was downright defamatory and had harmed her business. As a result, she took Liles to court, filing a $7,500 defamation lawsuit against him.

The court dismissed her case. To make matters worse, Liles was awarded $8,000 in attorney fees, $337 in costs, and $500 in what's called a prevailing party fee. Neumann, the business owner, immediately appealed the ruling, then Liles followed up with a counter-appeal to recover what he said was the full cost of his attorney's fees.

His counter-appeal was granted and the entire case made its way to the Oregon Supreme Court. Because Neumann could not afford her own representation for the Supreme Court hearing, she represented herself. At the hearing she likened Liles's reviews to a form of cyberbullying for businesses.

Perhaps you can relate to Neumann's actions. If a negative online review has harmed your business, you may have felt that clearing your name and punishing the reviewer were worthwhile reasons to have your day in court.

You may have been inspired by countless depictions on TV and in film that have dramatized criminals getting their comeuppance and victims being treated warmly by sympathetic judges and jurors. But rarely do those Hollywood portrayals represent the reality of the civil court system.

As the *Neumann v Liles* case shows, litigation is financially and emotionally costly. Perhaps most critically, however, the immense time required overseeing your case and navigating through an overburdened and underfunded court system will detract from your ability to focus on your business.

You might be feeling that a lawsuit is your final option, but I want to present you with two additional paths along the journey that involve appealing to a higher power for assistance—from the site itself or from outside reputation management companies that may be able to help you address the impact of the negative review.

Legal action would be the very last path to take.

Before you delve into the methods below, take a moment to reflect on all that you've learned in this book. Recall the *Manipurated* Code of Conduct (on page 55), where you committed to not taking things too personally.

Recall the Perfect Review Sandwich (see page 90), which gives you solid proof that the presence of a few negative reviews can actually improve your overall reputation. You might determine, after some soul searching, that your best course of action is to *leave the review alone* and focus on the tactics in Chapter 9 to start generating new reviews.

Nevertheless, I understand there are situations when a specific review has gone too far, beyond what is acceptable under any circumstances.

Path One: Work with the Site That Hosts the Review

Rating-and-review sites have argued vigorously that they maintain a neutral role in the business and consumer relationship. They don't take sides, mediate grievances, or determine right from wrong.

If you happen to be an auto dealer, there is a bit of good news, as DealerRater is an outlier to this industry rule. Its site has amassed nearly 2 million consumer reviews of auto dealers. When DealerRater receives a negative review about a business, it regularly mediates a resolution between the consumer and the dealer in question before the review is published.

Barring that single industry exception, nearly all other rating-and-review sites take an aggressively neutral stance when it comes to arbitrating disputes between reviewers and the businesses they reviewed.

So when *does* a rating-and-review site take action?

Common Rating-and-Review Site TOS Provisions

Rating-and-review sites will take action that may involve removing a review or suspending a reviewer if the contents of a review violate specific elements of their terms of service. The nature of the terms of service varies by site, but I have summarized the broad categories that would lead most rating-and-review sites to take action:

False Information

In general, this category is designed to filter reviews that have misleading information, such as incorrect store hours or location, describe the wrong business (perhaps a different location, or a different business of the same or similar name). These are generally resolved quickly in favor of the business owner.

Conflicts of Interest

Reviews that fall under this category are those written by individuals whose backgrounds call into question the neutrality of their perspectives. These include reviews written by ex-employees and competitors of the business being reviewed, or friends and family members of the business owner.

Most rating-and-review sites provide an area where you can describe why you believe the review reflects a conflict of interest. This will appear after you've clicked to flag the review.

It is helpful to be specific when submitting these details. If you can point to other reviews or information available online, you have a better chance at success. Can you demonstrate, via other reviews, that they have a verified conflict of interest?

Hate Speech or Threats

Reviews that contain bigoted language targeting a particular group of people, threatening language, or language that threatens the use of violence—verbal or physical—are subject to immediate removal. While some forms of cyberbullying fall within rating-and-review sites' acceptable-use standards, reviews containing hate speech or threats are ones rating-and-review sites will quickly remove.

Personal Information

Generally speaking, reviews that contain names, email addresses, phone numbers, home addresses, and other personal information of business owners or their employees are subject to prompt removal for privacy reasons.

Secondhand Accounts

This category of TOS violation is an exception to the others because it does not appear on every major rating-and-review site. Reviews that fall under this group reflect content not based on personal experience.

For instance, let's say a reviewer submitted the following on a hotel rating-and-review site:

My best friend stayed at the hotel and thought it was the worst place ever. She said she'll never go back!

A review written from this secondhand perspective will almost certainly be removed. On the other hand, if your complaint rests on a review you believe is *not* based on a real experience but the review doesn't explicitly express a secondhand account, you'll be hard pressed to convince the rating-and-review site to take action.

If you've determined that a review has crossed one of these boundaries, how do you persuade the site to do anything about it? Few of them have a customer service phone number, and they do their best to avoid contact with business owners.

Flag the Review

Your path to getting the attention of rating-and-review sites involves flagging a review. Most display a small flag icon or link that says "report review." You click on this link or icon to start the flagging process. You will generally be presented with a small window that asks you why you are reporting the review (using one of the TOS categories above) and gives you some space to provide supporting information. This supporting information is an important mechanism for getting action, so compose your thoughts and your words carefully. You won't have much space to write lengthy arguments.

Compose Your Compelling Argument

Here are some tips to making this short supporting statement stand out:

1. **Be precise.** Short, concise sentences stand the best chance of catching the attention of the site. Your request is likely to be scanned by someone reviewing a dizzying number of flag requests every single day. Make it stand out by being brief and precise, with no extraneous detail. Keep to the facts of the TOS violation.

2. **Don't Reinvent the Wheel.** Research the site's TOS. In the complaint you submit, refer to the content that is relevant to the TOS violation you're addressing.

3. **Provide Evidence.** If you simply flag a review based on an unsubstantiated hunch that it's inaccurate or written by a fake reviewer, the rating-and-review site will likely leave the review as is. But if you can provide evidence that the review is inaccurate or the reviewer is fake, you may convince the rating-and-review site to take action. You might include links to other reviews that substantiate your case.

4. **Stick to the Facts.** Don't worry about crafting elaborate arguments. Just stick to the facts, avoid sweeping statements ("I've never seen anything so egregious in my life!"), and be specific.

5. **Don't Be a Chronic Complainer.** Use the flag request sparingly and only when absolutely warranted and substantiated. Like the boy who cried wolf to the point no one believed him anymore, you don't want the rating-and-review site to come to view you as a chronic complainer. Fortunately, if you've followed what appears in this chapter so far, you know when your potential flag request is legitimate in the eyes of the rating-and-review site, and when it will be ignored.

When you flag a rating or review, this action typically triggers someone on the company's support team to screen it. At the very best, this person's assessment will be cursory. In the rare instance the rating-and-review site takes action, which may happen if the review blatantly violates the site's TOS, the review will be removed after a few days or weeks after you've flagged it.

Who Will Review Your Complaint?

Considering the amount of content that pours into rating-and-review sites everyday, you can imagine how many flagged ratings and reviews they receive.

Generally speaking, people on the user support team who review flagged reviews scan them in large batches. This means they do not investigate every flag request in detail. In addition, most of the time they're evaluating the review on the merits of its contents alone, and will not conduct further research. Therefore, the more specific and straightforward your remarks are, the higher the likelihood someone on the user support team will read your complaint.

Path Two: Hire a Reputation Management Company to Do Your Bidding

If questionable and stubborn reviews continue to threaten or thwart your business and you have struggled to address them, consider talking to an outside reputation management company. I addressed these companies in Chapter Four.

You need to choose carefully to ensure you are getting what you need out of the relationship and are getting a good value for the services rendered. There are plenty of good, legitimate organizations, just as there are plenty of shady reputation managements companies that will overcharge you for their services or utilize black hat SEO tactics.

Some of these organizations specialize in industries such as health care, automotive, or restaurants. To support your search for the right kind of provider, I present a ten-point questionnaire on page 134.

In addition, you may find that the best preventative measure to avoid scams is to follow news within your professional network. This was the case for the photographers I mentioned in Chapter Four, who learned through online discussions news of other photographers being targeted by a reputation management scam that threatened them with negative reviews.

To arm yourself with this knowledge for your own industry, subscribe to the following within your industry's professional organization or trade group:

- Email lists
- Discussion boards
- Blogs

Finding Reputation Management Companies

Your search for a reputation management company may begin on one of the industry-specific forums I just mentioned. After all, referrals from other business owners like you are valuable.

Your next best bet, in the absence of direct referrals, is a list from a company called TopSEOs, which maintains a database of SEO and reputation management companies.

Resource: www.topseos.com/rankings-of-best-reputation-management-companies

TopSEOs claims it is an independent source of SEO and reputation management vendor information, but there is some controversy in the industry about its methodology and practices. Therefore, use its list as a guide to your exploration of reputation management companies, then do your own due diligence to ensure your final list of candidates truly meets your needs.

The Reputation Management Relationship

Most reputation management companies price their services on a monthly fee basis, beginning as low as a few hundred dollars per month to thousands of dollars per month. These companies will generally talk to you about your broader online reputation, not just a specific negative review.

Often their tactics mirror some of the options already outlined in Chapter 9, particularly the companies offering review funnel software. A key tactic to overcoming negative reviews, after all, is to generate new reviews (freshness). Consider if one of those review funnel providers might be better suited to your needs, at a much lower cost.

Ten Questions to Ask Reputation Management Companies

1. How long have you been in business?
Ten years in business is far better than ten months—in other words, the longer the better.

2. Where are you located and how can I reach you?
Knowing where the consultant or business is located, and how you can get in touch, will help you avoid professional deadbeats. If the consultant or business is at all evasive in its answer, keep looking.

3. What tactics do you recommend for my business?
The consultant or company should describe things such as working on your website, content generation, and influencer reviews. If you hear anything related to creating "new reviews" or the tactics are unclear and confusing, this may be a sign of black hat practices.

4. Have you worked with others in my industry before? Can you provide any client referrals?
Contact the referrals and question them about their experience with the company.

5. How do you remove bad reviews from Yelp (or other review sites)?
This is an ethical test. The answer should always be "We can't. This isn't possible."

6. How long will it take before I start seeing results?
If the consultant claims it can deliver results in thirty days or less, it may be engaging in black hat tactics. Thirty days is a short turnaround. Legitimate reputation management is a long-term investment.

7. Will I be penalized by Google, Yelp, or TripAdvisor for anything you plan to do?
The prospective consultant should be able to clearly articulate how its tactics will not penalize you and how its white hat strategies comply with industry acceptability standards.

8. How often will you update me with a status report?
The timing of these reports should be up to you. The point of this question is to weed out companies that may disappear from the planet shortly after you've given them money. Inquire about what they'll share with you in the reports, and get them to commit to a reporting timeline that meets your needs.

9. How active are you in your industry? Do you speak at conferences?
This question has to do with credibility within the reputation management industry. Take note if the consultant can point you to a presentation it gave or a panel discussion it participated in at a major industry event, or an article it published in a major publication.

10. Optional: Can you tell me about a time you've struggled with your own reputation, and what you did about it?
This one is a bit like the "Tell me about your weaknesses" question in a job interview. A good consultant or reputation management company will be able to describe a time when it had to deal with its own reputation management predicament. Sooner or later, everyone experiences critics. It's the response that counts, more than the criticism itself.

Reputation management companies may also talk with you about your SERPs (Search Engine Results Pages), customer email, website, and other online marketing channels.

You should be prepared to provide these organizations with access to any website analytics you might have (like Google Analytics) and details about negative reviews, including access to your merchant/business account on the rating-and-review site.

Path Three: Turn to Litigation as a Last Resort

Imagine you're a small business owner who is a victim of a negative or fake rating or review posted by an anonymous reviewer. Or let's say a rating or review you receive is inaccurate and you want the rating-and-review site to remove it.

So you flag the review and submit an impeccably crafted complaint. To your dismay, the rating-and-review site turns a blind eye. Next, you hire a reputation management company to try to bury the fake review with new, fresh reviews, and that tactic also fails.

Now you decide to take the rating-and-review site to court. You've already lost time by flagging the review and money by hiring a reputation management company. At this juncture, fully infuriated, you believe that the legal system may offer you some relief and at least some of your dignity back.

If past performance is any indication of future returns, the likelihood is the legal system will not offer you much resolution.

So my question to you is this:

Is it worth risking your business, your savings, your livelihood, and your mental well-being in order to have your day in court?

That's the road you'll take when you explore legal action. The day in court you envision may result in losing your case, which means the legal precedent your case establishes will favor the rating-and-review industry.

That said, if you've come this far and feel this is your last hope at salvaging your business, righting the grievance, and recovering lost income, I provide you below with a short road map to the documentation you'll be expected to provide to the attorney you select. Start gathering these documents at the first gut feeling that you might end up in a legal battle.

- Document communications with the reviewer, including dates and times, what was said and by whom.
- Take screenshots of everything, and check often for changes; reviewers can alter or change their review after it is published, so be certain you're getting the entire chain of events. Take care to get dates on the screenshots, which are often next to or underneath the review.
- Take careful notes of the steps you've taken to remediate the situation, including flagging the review, any response from the rating-and-review site, and any communication you had with anyone regarding addressing the review.
- Document, to the best of your ability, lost revenue directly related to the review—this may involve customers telling you they chose to shop elsewhere, decided against using your services due to a review, or even recommended other businesses over yours.
- Look for the tribe mentality—sometimes, you may find that one negative review leads to another. A common scenario would be a negative review about a specific product or service ("The lobster ravioli was the worst experience of my entire life") which then is followed by negative reviews from other customers ("As Poster ABC said, the lobster ravioli really WAS the worst experience of my life").

These elements will likely be among the first things an attorney asks to see regarding your potential case, and it will benefit you to have documented everything along the way rather than trying to go back and piece it together later.

No matter the path you take in seeking a higher power to help you resolve harmful reviews, know that your customers are generally on your side. You may start to feel that it is "me vs. them," but in reality you've learned that most consumers see negative and hateful reviews in a bigger context. What may feel like a cause for panic to you is likely just seen as another day on the crazy Internet by your consumers.

From the Source: A Q&A with Yelp's Darnell Holloway

In my research for Manipurated, I interviewed business owners across the country. During our discussions, they shared similar concerns and questions about online rating-and-review sites. I spoke with Darnell Holloway, Yelp's director of Local Business Outreach, and asked him to address these frequently asked questions.

Q: Is there any way to remove a business from Yelp altogether?

A: Holloway says, "The only way to remove a business is to close or move to a new location." He explained that anyone can add a business to Yelp, including the business owner and consumer. Yelp also receives data from third-party sources (Axiom is one example). By the way, this is standard practice for most local listing services, including Google My Business.

My Manipurated Tip: If you remove your business in one database, it will likely just reappear due to data coming from another source. As you know, it's very challenging to disappear on the Internet. So the short answer, as Holloway noted, is no.

Q: How does a business owner reach Yelp?

A: Holloway says if you're a Yelp advertiser you will have a dedicated account manager. This person is the single point of contact (there is no central customer support number). All businesses, regardless of their status with Yelp, can reach the company at www.yelp.com/support.

Q: What are the best ways for businesses to generate Yelp reviews?

A: Holloway detailed three key pillars of earning a successful reputation on the platform:

1. Provide good customer service.
2. Practice consistent and diplomatic responses to customer reviews.

3. Leave a trail of breadcrumbs. In other words, steps that make it easy for your customers to find you on Yelp, including window clings, business cards, mentions on receipts (Find us on Yelp!), and more.

Q: For a new business, what are the best ways to increase visibility on Yelp?

A: The recommendations Holloway provided also apply to most businesses, not just new ones. The following are a few steps to take:

1. Put a Yelp badge on your website to make it clear you're on the site.
2. Set up a **check-in** offer to increase your customers' engagement with your business on the site. This means when customers check into your business on Yelp, the next time they log in to the Yelp site they're presented with a reminder to leave you a review. Setting this up is free, so you don't have to spend money on Yelp to test this out for your business. You can also offer a variety of incentives for check-ins such as buy-one-get-one-free deals or discounts.
3. Leave a trail of breadcrumbs, including storefront signage, Yelp logos on takeout menus and business cards, and a Yelp badge on your website.
4. Holloway also suggests double-checking that all of the current information about your business is accurate by claiming your business at biz.yelp.com. Be sure the hours, contact information, and details about amenities are accurate and up-to-date.

Q: Should businesses respond to every single review on Yelp?

A: Holloway says all business should have "some sort of response strategy." This doesn't necessarily mean you must address every single review. Holloway suggests responding to a mix of positive and negative reviews. By doing so, you're establishing a relationship with the customer.

Q: How much time should a business realistically expect to spend on Yelp reviews?
A: Holloway says this is highly subjective. For multilocation businesses, it could be several hours per week.

My *Manipurated* Tip: Jump to the *Manipurated* 20-Minute Quick Start Guide on page 142 for a starting point.

Q: What should I do if I suspect a business is stuffing its ratings and reviews with fake content?
A: Holloway described three elements to Yelp's system:

1. **Software:** The Yelp algorithm generates scores based on its reviewers' quality, reliability, and their activity. Yelp's algorithm may pick up fake, biased, or friends-and-family reviews, as well as ones from the same IP address.

2. **Consumer alerts:** As a warning to customers, these are placed directly on the business's profile page. Consumer alerts indicate a business is suspected of falsifying its reviews.

3. **Flag:** When specific items are flagged, this means they have been or currently are being evaluated by the user support team. If the review violates the terms and conditions of the site, it will be removed. Some examples that meet the flagging threshold include the following content:
   - Does it reference firsthand experience ("I ate here … " versus "My friend said he ate there")?
   - Is it by a disgruntled ex-employee or does it demonstrate a conflict of interest?
   - Does it contain threatening or hate speech or personal information?

Conclusion

You probably started reading this book due to a specific situation that you faced in your business. You came to *Manipurated* to solve a problem, and I hope the book helped you confront it.

I also hope it gave you a larger perspective on managing your business reputation. Ratings and reviews are one component in a very complex equation. But you have seen now why the industry is structured the way it is, with an emphasis on fresh content and high volumes of reviews. You now understand how these factors influence and affect your business, and you know precisely what you can do about it. I hope you've internalized, through all of the case studies, that there is reason to be optimistic about how ratings and reviews impact your business—whether you are a dentist, a gondola tour operator, car dealer, lawyer, moving company owner, or restauranteur.

No doubt, managing ratings and reviews is tough. It is an industry where the only constant is change.

I'm keeping track of these changes on my site, **www.manipurated.com**, which I hope you will visit.

There you will find up-to-the-minute tips and advice on the latest trends, techniques, and news you need to know. There you will also find a free email newsletter filled with great content.

Keeping you informed and educated is my passion. I hope you'll let me know how I can better serve you, and I look forward to hearing from you and sharing in your success. You can reach me on Twitter **@ daniellemin**, or if you prefer by email, **daniel@manipurated.com**.

Manipurated 20-Minute Quick Start Guide

Your Daily Rating-and-Review Healthy Habits Start Here:

☐ **New Reviews (2 minutes)**
Check for new reviews as a first step every single day. You can use one of the review gathering tools from this book or look directly on your top rating-and-review sites.

☐ **Review the Reviews (5 minutes)**
What do the new reviews say? Are there suggestions for improvements, or did something go awry yesterday unexpectedly? Gather insight from the reviews, then forward their contents to anyone else in your company who needs to see them.

☐ **Draft Your Answers (10 minutes)**
First, practice Wade Lombard's *Stop, Drop, and Roll* method (see Chapter 8). Then, draft answers to the reviews that were posted. If you're concerned about the tone or tenor of a particular response, it's best to ask someone for feedback before posting it. Otherwise, post your response.

☐ **Cross-Promote the Best Reviews (3 minutes)**
Did someone say something truly exceptional? After thanking the reviewer, write a quick status update on your Facebook page with a link to the review, or include it in an email you're drafting.

In just twenty minutes each day, you'll be on your way to a more satisfying review experience that will benefit your business.

Index

Acknowledgements

· ·

No book ever makes it to the printer without a giant community of contributors. I have many people to thank for helping me bring this project to life. These people understood the harsh reality that businesses face online and joined me to create *Manipurated*.

Steven Tan, who above all patiently supported my quest to create this book. His energy and enthusiasm for the subject manifests throughout the book, including in the title. Without him, I'd still be on page one. I never could have done it without him.

Jay Baer, who supported the project from our first conversation at a restaurant in Laguna Beach and never fails to be a connector or sounding board. His input and support was essential to this entire project.

Kent Sorsky at Quill Driver Books, who saw the potential for this book and invested his own time and energy to make the project happen, and offered many words of wisdom to an anxious first-time author.

Bobby Boas, the inspiration for the book from its earliest days. His story was the catalyst that caused me to put the outline together.

Lawrence Ineno, my editor. His expertise and creative solutions were a godsend, and his endless positive energy helped make this one of the most fulfilling professional projects of my career.

Lisa Loeffler, who helped me refine this book many times, continues to lend her expertise to make sure as many people as possible see its message.

Kim Corak, the queen of dynamic book concepts who helped me frame the marketing approach to the book.

Krys Grondorf, for her battle against my repeated overuse of commas, and her genuine support.

Chris Campbell at Review Trackers, who gave advice early on and helped guide my research efforts.

The team at Convince & Convert—Kelly Santina, Chris Sietsema, Zontee Hou, Megan Gilbert—all of whom offered tons of free advice and comments when the book was in the proposal stage and continue to help make it better.

Bob Weinstein, who helped me research and assemble a winning book proposal.

Allan Duong and San Nguyen at Hamilton, DeSanctis & Cha, who were instrumental in securing the *Manipurated* trademark carried on this book.

Dr. Steve Iseman, who I've considered a mentor since my undergraduate days, and who taught me to never stop searching for stories worth telling.

And a whole extended family of colleagues who encouraged me to pursue this: **Jean Gonsoulin, Jessica Payne, Adam Freed, Karen Wickre, Barry Schnitt, Maggie Habib, Debbie Frost, Matthew Bautista, Jon Cronin, Ryan Sievers and many others.**

And finally my family, particularly my mother **Diana Lemin**, who provided early editorial guidance on my book proposal and taught me that you should stick with something once you start.

Never Be Manipurated Again!

Now that you've read *Manipurated*, visit **Manipurated.com** to learn more about how to leverage online rating-and-review sites.

You'll find free resources, including ebooks, videos, and tutorials. The site also features product reviews and articles that will support your online marketing strategy.

You'll also find case studies that reflect the experiences of business owners—just like you. You'll relate to their pitfalls, learn from their mistakes, and draw guidance and inspiration from their triumphs.

At Manipurated.com, you can order additional copies for friends and family. In addition, *Manipurated* is available at your favorite online booksellers.

Lastly, if you're interested in having him speak at your next event, click on "Speaking and Consulting" at Manipurated.com. There, you'll also find information about Daniel's consulting services and workshops he leads for organizations throughout the country.

You can get in touch with Daniel:

Web: www.manipurated.com
Twitter: @daniellemin
Email: daniel@manipurated.com

About the Author

Daniel Lemin is a respected authority on the reputation industry. An early Google hire, Lemin was one of the first pioneers to realize the importance, impact, and power of online ratings and reviews on small businesses and the ongoing struggle business owners have with their online reputations. Lemin is an acknowledged expert on digital marketing, public relations, and reputation management and is a consultant for prominent Fortune 500 companies, including Nestlé USA, Procter & Gamble, Hilton Hotels, Sony, Suzuki Motors, Munchkin, and Best Buy. Lemin is also a senior strategist with the consulting firm Convince & Convert, a regular contributor to the Convince & Convert marketing blog, rated the number-one content-marketing blog in the world, and a frequent speaker at industry events and trade shows. Lemin holds an M.A. in communications and leadership from Gonzaga University.